"Mike Stavlund invites us into the story of ... W9-BYA-904 and fury, with beauty and violence, and it feels like a holy privilege to witness his grief. If you've had your heart broken beyond imagination, and you feel desperately alone in your mourning, you will find your kinsman in these pages."

Shauna Niequist, author of *Bittersweet* and *Bread and Wine*

"This book is about life in all its splendor and in all its agony. Mike talks about pain without trying to theologize it away. His book rips your heart out—it's raw, honest, and rare—a book on grief that isn't fluffy and neat, because life isn't fluffy and neat. But Mike's book is true, and truth sets us free, even though it may leave us with some scars. Mike reminds us that we have a God familiar with pain, who is ready to meet us in ours. Even Jesus cried out, 'My God, My God, why have you forsaken me?' Mike Stavlund reminds us that it's okay for us to feel darkness—for even in our darkest moments we are not alone. And that is good news to all."

Shane Claiborne, author and activist (thesimpleway.org)

"Mike Stavlund's *A Force of Will* gives voice to love, to love entwined with grief, to grief evoked by love, to love for a tiny imperfectly formed infant and grief upon his death. It is concrete, gripping, unflinchingly honest, theologically and psychologically probing, beautifully written— a tribute to tiny Will and a model of how to live with grief in faith."

Nicholas Wolterstorff, Noah Porter Emeritus Professor of Philosophical Theology at Yale University

"Stavlund's record of the birth, brief life, and abrupt death of his infant son is an unguarded account of a parental agony totally lacking in self-protection. As such, it can be a wrenching read in places, but it is also one that you will neither put down unfinished nor soon forget. It is a skillful, clear, beautifully rendered memoir."

Phyllis Tickle, founding editor of the Religion Department at *Publishers Weekly*

"Mourning is impossible; if it succeeds, you forget; if it does not succeed, you cannot move on. Mike Stavlund embraces this dilemma head-on by way of writing—spilling out the whole thing, speaking the unspeakable in a beautiful, eloquent and moving narrative that is both deeply personal and theologically resonant. *A Force of Will* proves once again, if we needed proof, that love and pain are inseparable and that there are bits of heaven sprinkled all over hell."

John D. Caputo, The Thomas J. Watson Professor of Religion Emeritus, Syracuse University

"*A Force of Will* is not just a book—it is an invitation into a new way of life. Mike Stavlund opens his life and the transformative pain he has experienced as guide to all who have struggled and suffered—you do not walk alone. This book is honest, hard, compelling and propelling. It sends us into our own lives and the world as new people."

Doug Pagitt, pastor, author, and radio host

"*A Force of Will* cannot be evaluated, appreciated, or interacted with at arm's length. Mike Stavlund writes about the loss of his son with such an unprotected heart and superb craft that readers are compelled to experience his grief, if only for a moment. I found myself grappling with loss and God's goodness even though I knew Mike's loss was not my own. Mike's honesty gives readers permission to abandon theological expectations of how grief should be experienced and to accept it on its own horrible terms."

Larry Shallenberger, pastor and author

"When you sense that an author is experiencing healing through his or her writing, you are likely to experience the same in your reading. This book combines this sense of healing with depth of insight, intensity of emotion, and beauty of style, which is why I consider it a true gift and an unforgettable read."

Brian D. McLaren, author, speaker, and activist (brianmclaren.net)

"Loss is common to all humanity. Still, no loss compares to the loss of a child. Mike and Stacy Stavlund have regrettably known that loss, but in an act of unfathomable grace they have shared with us their grief and pursuit of a faith that could endure. In so doing, they give those of us who may never know such loss a faith-filled example for bearing our own losses—whatever they may be—in ways that make us more fully human."

Melvin Bray, storyteller, educator, and Emmy Award-winning writer

"Our pain before God is not alien; it is inseparable from the journey of faith, a journey upon which Mike serves as our trusted guide. He invites us to confront the full spectrum of emotions to which grief calls us, to face them as we face God—not just with fear and trembling, but with courage and grace."

Logan Mehl-Laituri, author, student at Duke Divinity School

"Mike Stavlund is a forceful writer, a passionate soul poured out on the page. His words will move you. His story will transport you. This memoir of a year of grief is a gift to us all who have experienced pain, are in the midst of it now, or will be soon enough. In the middle of my own season of grief, Mike's story brought me to tears, made me laugh, and took me to another place—into his story and his pain and out of my own, even just for a little while."

Steve Knight, Co-Founder and Co-CEO, SogoMedia.TV

"This book is a psalm: cries of hope and praise, bottomless wails of grief and lament, accusatory anger, disillusioned weakness, exhausted surrender, and always, always, wrestling with God. There's no tidy ending—just the force of will to move forward. Therefore, it is a work of hope."

Tony Jones, author, Theologian-in-Residence at Solomon's Porch

"As a Palliative Care physician, the journey towards death is one that I walk with many children and families. I've been to the place where all else has failed, where we are left only with our fragile hope and the gnawing fear that God will remain silent. Mike Stavlund meets us in this place and gives us a beautifully raw account of a father's struggle with the loss of his son. While this is understandably a book of grief, and anger, and doubt, it is primarily a book about the fullness of life, and of finding peace in the darkest of places. I read this book aloud, delighting in Mike's voice in every page and poem. And I wept aloud because, in some strange way, I too mourned the loss of this precious child. A Force of Will offers a message desperately needed by the Church—the journey may be painful and is not yet done, but we have a suffering God who walks this road with us, even through death."

Michael D. Barnett, MD, MS, Assistant Professor of Medicine & Pediatrics, University of Alabama at Birmingham

"This is the kind of brutal honesty we all need—especially those of us who have been hurt and are hurting deeply. Stavlund's honesty pushes us to ask aloud our uncomfortable questions about God and God's response to our suffering. Not only does Stavlund say God is present in our suffering, but in suffering our true theology emerges. We desperately need theologies that sustain us, not those whose 'answers' defeat us. I highly recommend this book!"

Thomas Jay Oord, Professor of Theology and Philosophy, Northwest Nazarene University

"How does one make meaning out of so much grief? In this book, Mike delves deep into the fiber of living painfully and courageously. Refusing sentimentality, A Force of Will is a narrative about the glorious rawness of love and the danger of being alive."

Eliacín Rosario-Cruz, Pastoral Leader, Church of the Apostles

"A Force of Will is a breath of fresh air for those who have ever grieved unspeakable losses within a community that was well-meaning but less than helpful, or among friends or family who offered simplistic answers. It reminds us that sometimes our presence among the grieving is all that needs to be 'said' . . . and love can be demonstrated through simple silence in someone's wordless pain. My prayer is that through

Will's story, they also may have the courage to share their stories in safe and supportive places and find healing for the journey ahead."

Kymberlee Stanley, Licensed Clinical Social Worker

"Mike Stavlund's *A Force of Will* is a stunning cinematic journey through one of the most challenging legs of the human story: accepting loss and becoming aware of the deep beauty that was ever-present. This is beautiful storytelling about loss, beauty, God, life and death. A marathon reminder to us all that the truth of whatever matters is never resolved or concluded but continually, willfully discovered and rediscovered in humility, grief, acceptance, negotiation and a surrender to life in all its arduous turns, hills, slopes and valleys."

Anthony Smith (aka PostmodernNegro), activist, pastor, and writer

"Mike's wonderfully written book is a beautiful tribute to his son, William, providing an accurate and thoughtful discussion of the way loss and grief change your relationship with everything around you—your family, your friends, and your faith. As someone who has worked in the medical social work field for over ten years, I would recommend this book without reservation to families experiencing a loss and to members of the medical team who also struggle with similar questions when a patient dies."

Heather Langlois, LICSW, Children's National Heart Institute

"A searing, soul-rending work of beauty that had me weeping. Besides being impossibly well written given the conditions, this book feels pure (or perhaps it is raw gold); it forcefully surges directly from the heart with a clarity gained by fire. Grant magisterial attention to those whose hearts have been pierced: as Jesus' heart was speared and the sacraments of the Church flowed from his side, Stavlund's unbearable burden of Will's holy heart brings us to the unfathomable burden of God's being. If not to tend to our past wounds, we need this book because we all share Mother Mary's grievous fate: 'a sword shall pierce your own heart also.'"

Chris Haw, carpenter, theologian, author, and potter

"In *A Force of Will*, Mike Stavlund courageously invites us into his personal story of grief and loss. With ruthless honesty and perceptive self-awareness he explores the struggles and the 'why' questions asked by anyone who has lost a loved one—especially a child. For the grieving person who has been hurt by well-meaning but candy-coated platitudes, this book offers a knowing realism about death that is surprisingly hopeful. The best new book on grief and loss, told with a father's heart and a poet's ear."

Mark Scandrette, author of *Soul Graffiti*
and *Practicing the Way of Jesus*

A FORCE OF WILL

The Reshaping of Faith in a Year of Grief

Mike Stavlund

BakerBooks

a division of Baker Publishing Group
Grand Rapids, Michigan

© 2013 by Mike Stavlund

Published by Baker Books
a division of Baker Publishing Group
P.O. Box 6287, Grand Rapids, MI 49516-6287
www.bakerbooks.com

Printed in the United States of America

Library of Congress Cataloging-in-Publication Data
Stavlund, Mike.
    A force of will : the reshaping of faith in a year of grief / Mike Stavlund.
        p.   cm.
    Includes bibliographical references (p.   ).
    ISBN 978-0-8010-1511-3 (pbk. : alk. paper)
    1. Children—Death—Religious aspects—Christianity. 2. Grief—Religious aspects—Christianity. 3. Stavlund, Mike. I. Title.
BV4907.S67 2013
248.8′66—dc23   2012034439

The internet addresses, email addresses, and phone numbers in this book are accurate at the time of publication. They are provided as a resource. Baker Publishing Group does not endorse them or vouch for their content or permanence.

The poem "Ella Elisabeth" by Mark A. Scandrette, © 2007 (section: Baptism Poems), is used with permission.

The lyrics for "Brighter Skies, an Advent Song" by Ryan Lee Sharp, © 2007 (section: Brighter Skies), are used with permission.

Cover design and illustration by SharpSeven Design

Author is represented by MacGregor Literary, Inc.

13 14 15 16 17 18 19   7 6 5 4 3 2 1

For William Addison Stavlund,
the strongest person I have ever known

And for everyone with the courage
to allow their experience of life
to change their understanding of God,
and who begin to see weakness
as a kind of strength

Contents

Acknowledgments

Thanks to:

Shelley Pagitt, who loved our family from afar, who compelled her husband to challenge me to write this book, who encouraged me along the way, and who enthusiastically read it in its entirety when it was complete.

Sheryl Fullerton, who with great kindness and pastoral sensitivity told a grieving father that she wasn't at all interested in publishing his book, but who never flagged in her support and encouragement and keen editorial insight.

Phyllis Tickle, the gentle literary giant who frightened and honored me by asking to read the manuscript, and whose weighty approval blessed me with both a burden and a freedom. To call her a friend is a great honor.

Sandra Bishop, who was excited to represent me, and who was persistent in her efforts through all of the twists and turns of finding our publisher. She is a fierce literary agent and a fine friend.

Amy Moffitt, who read the manuscript no fewer than three times and was an energetic supporter ever after. If confidence is the fuel in a writer's life, then Amy has been following me with a tanker truck for four years.

Holly Sharp, who has inspired me with her friendship and artistry and painting, and who was kind enough not only to design the cover but allow me to feel as if I was contributing to the process.

Jon Wilcox, who was a double blessing. As acquisitions editor, he saw the potential in my manuscript and gave it a home. As editor, he encouraged me and pressed me to make my work much better. Being assigned an editor is a scary proposition, but Jon was the pot at the end of the rainbow.

Jon White, who read the manuscript, then determined to give me a professional website. Which has felt like a comfortable home and a proper place to launch further writing ventures. It is a great compliment when an artist not only gives you a beautiful tool but a new vision of yourself.

Doug Pagitt, whose greatest gift to the world is just being Doug. Ply many widely respected Christian leaders with a beverage and inquire after the most empowering person they know, and Doug will be at the top of the list. His friendship has been a confidence and a catalyst for me in many ways.

And of course to my beloved wife, Stacy (Sparks) Stavlund, who walked with me through everything, and who resolutely sent me out the door at least once a week to write, full of faith in the importance of this story. When she was finally able to read it five years later, I only needed to hear her say "It's good" to find my peace.

There are many relational threads that tie this book together: Troy Bronsink introduced me to Jon Irvine, who talked to Mike Morrell, who submitted my proposal to Chip MacGregor of MacGregor Literary. Chip casts a mighty long shadow in the literary world, so I was elated to learn that he had appreciated my manuscript and passed it on to his colleague Sandra Bishop.

Common Table is my church home, and a community for which I'm ever grateful. I wasn't easy to live with in my grief, but they never ran away, or backed down, or pushed back. Instead, they loved me, forgave me, and taught me how to grieve. And they love and honor my son even to this day.

Many thanks to the trusted readers of earlier drafts of the book: Jackie Bulanow, Mike Croghan, Jen Kloss, Deanna Doan, Tim Hartmann, Kate Maisel, stealth reader Pete Stavlund, and that random guy in an Atlanta pub who somehow got ahold of the manuscript and gushed to me about it (sometimes lush praise is the most sincere form of flattery).

Every book has a place. I wrote most of this one at Murky, the infamous, excellent, and proudly independent coffee shop, where stellar coffee combined with worn plywood floors to create the perfect palate for personal exploration. It now exists only in memory, replaced by a much fancier place with a more grim and upbeat clientele, but it was the ideal incubator for my writing.

Every book has a soundtrack. This one was written with BT and Radiohead in my ears, and The Cobalt Season, The Psalters, the everybodyfields, and Bruce Springsteen on my mind. Edits were aided by Rosanne Cash's incredible work on grief, *Black Cadillac*; Son Lux; Gillian Welch; and of course more Radiohead. If you want to know what this book sounds like, play their albums *Kid A* and *OK Computer*.

Many books were jettisoned during the year I wrote this, but a few became precious: Dave Eggers's *A Heartbreaking Work of Staggering Genius*; Joan Didion's *The Year of Magical Thinking*; Nicholas Wolterstorff's *Lament for a Son*; and John Caputo's *The Weakness of God*. Bill McKibben's greatest work, *Long Distance: A Year of Living Strenuously*, became even more beloved. And Alan Wolfelt's wonderful collection of grief resources was invaluable as well.

To my family, living and dead, near and far, close and distant, in-law and outlaw, I am thankful for all of our connections and laughter and memories and collective wisdom, but most of all for the love.

And finally, many thanks and much love to my favorite girls and brightest lights, Eleanor, Lucia, and Miriam. I am deeply grateful for our life together.

Mike Stavlund
Lent, 2012

Preface

Fifteen miles. This is the part of the Boston Marathon where things get quiet. The crowds dwindle in this less residential area as spectators jump on the train to catch a ride to the finish line. On the course itself, the population of runners seems to decrease too, as masses of sweaty bodies give way to solitary figures and loosely organized groups trying to share the work of pushing against the headwind. We runners talk less as our eyes settle into a middle-distance stare and we try not to think the menacing thought: *eleven miles to go*. Of course, if our muscles made noises, this would be where the volume increased. We'd hear squawks and complaints and foreboding protests. But we can't or won't pay attention. At least not yet.

My presence here—the chance to run, to indulge in months of obsessive preparation and training—is a gift from my wife. A kind respite from eighteen months of speculation and assessment of our respective reproductive systems as we dig ever deeper into learning why we are unable to become pregnant. A break from round after round of stressful and invasive infertility treatments. A chance to pull back and reconsider whether our desire to be parents is overwhelming our better judgment; whether we might best lay down our hopes and dreams and embrace our current life of just the two of us. The marathon is, in spite of all appearances, an escape.

And it certainly is a distraction, on a massive scale. Twenty thousand runners have come here from all over the world after earning a spot by running another marathon fast enough to qualify for this one. So when we walked through the convention center to pick up our race information, our coveted T-shirts, and the numbers that we've pinned to our chests, it was with a fair bit of pride. We've *earned this*, by some combination of the sweat of our brow and the strength of our character and force of luck. We've weaved our way through injuries, inhospitable weather, dark mornings, snowy streets, wet shoes, withering training runs, family obligations, piles of pasta, uncooperative schedules, and our own doubts.

We've traveled to this great city and watched as billboards, street signs, and bus placards rolled by our vision, paying homage to our presence here. We've eaten one last meal, mouthed our way through one final bedtime bagel, and tried our best to sleep. In the morning, we've awakened with special gravity, checked our gear one last time, and walked to Boston Common, where an endless line of yellow school buses wait to take us on the one-way trip to Hopkinton, twenty-six miles away. We've ridden the bus, felt the adrenaline coursing through it, and stolen glances at those seated around us while quietly wondering about their stories, their journeys, their intended and actual outcomes today. Most of all, we've tried to ignore the very plain fact that this forty-minute bus ride means we have a very, very long way to run this afternoon.

The place where we runners muster to while away the hours before we head to the starting line is dubbed "Athletes' Village." A large tent city assembled on the grounds of a high school, it is a place to find some distraction by socializing, napping, reading, or waiting in the Porta-John line to relieve your nervous and overly hydrated bladder. The first time I came here, the energy and excitement was too much, and so I retreated to the tree line at the edge of the property, where I sat down with a book, leaned against an oak, and tried to pretend I was somewhere else. Several days later, when the rash on my lower back kept getting worse, I realized I had also leaned against some poison ivy.

But this year I rode the bus with a couple of friends, and met a couple more in Hopkinton. They are training partners from my home in Washington, DC, who had met up on many predawn winter mornings to push and pull each other through our longer workouts. Now we sat on the grass in the spring sun, talked about how hot it was, and did our best to adjust our goals accordingly.

Then, at 11:30, we made the slow walk to the starting line, nervously joking as we passed through this quiet residential neighborhood toward the circus atmosphere of the starting area. Once there, we were segregated into corrals based on our qualifying times, where we waited even more. Gathered inside these fences, no one says much, and no one looks into anyone's eyes. We just nod absently at each other and allow whatever peculiarities seem necessary. There will be some pacing, some jogging in place, some stretching, and some staring off into space. Some folks will be wearing tattered rags that must be considered lucky, and others will be decked out in crisp clothes bearing the emblem of this very race. In this mass of peculiar and desperate humanity, things like squatting in the street to relieve oneself are absolutely acceptable: we runners are a fierce and strange tribe.

I pace around in aimless, irregular circles, feeling a heavy weight on my shoulders and a lightness in my steps, and my mind pulses with the last song I heard on the bus, BT's aptly

17

titled "Knowledge of Self," and its lyric "ready to go, ready to go, let my energy flow . . ."

What follows is familiar to anyone who has participated in a marathon. First, there is the warbled singing of the national anthem, followed by a smattering of applause from the less distracted runners, followed by the steady press of bodies pushing forward in their respective corrals. Then there is some indecipherable announcement over a badly tuned PA system, and then the sound of a gun firing. Feet shuffle, then stride, then break into a familiar pace as the roar of the crowd draws us down Highway 135.

The emotional rush that pushes any runner through the first ten miles of a marathon is multiplied in Boston by the crowd of one hundred thousand spectators, as well as the general drop in elevation as the course winds its way through Ashland and Framingham. There are ups and downs, to be sure, but the overwhelming sense is that one is being *pulled along* by both emotion and gravity. With proper training and pacing, the first ten miles can pass under one's feet almost effortlessly, leaving the euphoric runner feeling as though no energy has been expended, and thinking, *Wow, I might be having the best race of my life.*

You're not, of course. Sometimes slowly, sometimes suddenly, but always and inevitably this emotional phase gives way to a physical one somewhere after ten miles. Keeping the pace now requires intentional effort, and we begin to be more diligent about grabbing an extra Gatorade from the yellow-jacketed volunteers staffing the water stations, and gulping down the bits of food that we have carried with us. Over and against our months of self-propagandizing, we're beginning to realize that this will be a long and difficult journey. Still, by leaning forward slightly and applying a little more physical force to the task, the pace can be maintained and worries about the finish can be pushed back.

But one's physicality must find some limit, too. Our bodies have only so much to give, and somewhere around fifteen miles our limitations can no longer be ignored. Muscles begin to knot into cramps—some in expected places like thighs and calves, but even more ominously in spots like arms and shoulders and necks. The fatigue is almost tangible as our energy reserves dwindle. Our legs seem leaden and our feet feel flat, devoid of any bounce. Our bodies are shutting down, in large ways and small. And so, though starved for oxygen, we call on our brains to push us through. After physicality fades, our mental faculties take over, doing their best to tune out this chorus of doubt and negativity and to limit our mental purview to but one section, one mile, one hill at a time.

In Boston, a mile-long winding menace named "Heartbreak Hill" gets all the notoriety, but I find an earlier incline to be the greater mental challenge. Cruising down from the village of Wellesley and the deafening screams of the historic all-women's university there, runners cross an exposed highway overpass before the course joins with Route 16 and heads up the less-famous "Hospital Hill." The first extended incline—and dark harbinger of many more to come—it stretches up past Newton-Wellesley Hospital, where some of the staff will have moved stretchers out to the curb as if to tempt runners to *give up, lie down, come inside.* Indeed, at a point in the race where quitting seems sensible and where death can seem preferable to life, passing by this place can be intimidating. The increasingly addled brain and withering body seem, in that moment, to easily qualify one for admission. And after all, a hospital admission might be the only way to save face with the family and friends who are watching your progress on the race website, and waiting to hear about the race. *Just give up*, the trees whisper, *and stop this madness.* But then rationality grabs the wheel again, and drives one up and over this incline, and toward the rest of the ominous hills of Newton waiting behind it. Until the great Heartbreak is finally crested five miles later and things change again.

Cruising down the back side of Heartbreak Hill, one can feel energized and exultant. The worst of the hills are behind, the great city of Boston opens to view, and an invigorating cool breeze blows off the harbor. Most important, the psychologically imposing twenty-mile mark has been crossed. But even as the runners descend the back side of the monster, hope can dwindle. For there are still *five miles* to go, with no apparent resources left to meet the task. At this point in the race, spectators still shout, but the emotional receptors of the runners are closed. By force of habit, runners attempt to lengthen their strides as they move down the hill, only to find that their legs don't stretch, not anymore. Desperate, they try to engage their dwindling mental faculties to muster a plan of action, but find that a dense fog has settled over the brain. As the road stretches out before you, it can feel as if you are running through a long tunnel while the sides are slowly, inexorably closing in.

This is what the Boston Marathon is all about. This is where we come to the end of ourselves, where volition alone moves us forward. This is the realm of *will.*

Nothing matters now. There is nothing you can eat, nothing that will help you. Go ahead and drop any snacks you've carried, for they will only slow you down now. It is too late to profitably drink anything, and besides, infinitesimally altering one's stride to reach out at a water stop would invite massive leg cramps. Not that a knot in your leg would change anything; if you are cramping now—and everyone is—there's no point in stopping to stretch or walk. If your leg seizes up and you stumble to keep from landing on your chin, then you'll just stagger in a palsied display until you stutter-step into a jog again. Your body seems torn between utter exhaustion and mysterious determination, and your brain seems detached as you notice your breath passing back and forth across your lips, as if propelled by some outside force. Where spectators once celebrated and shouted at the runners en masse, they now seem driven by some unspoken personal obligation to help. They look into the empty stares of individual runners and implore, *Keep going! You can make it!*—though everyone, runners and spectators alike, wonders if this is true.

Here and now, if you are moving, it is because you are being driven by your will. And *this* is why I am here, I remember. This is why I keep running, keep training, keep testing myself in these completely arbitrary courses of 26.2 miles. This is why I keep doing this thing that I don't actually enjoy. For here, I am stripped down to my true self. Here, I am a body, and I am a soul, and I am nothing more. I am, all at once, a hollow shell, and the fullest expression of my glorious humanity—the *imago dei*. My many layers of pretense and defense are gone now. A lifetime of education and socialization falls away, and I am just me. My simplest self, my soul, my naked will.

One year and one month later, I will be feeling all of this again when I rest my hand on the tiny hospital bed of my three-pound son. I will watch him struggle to breathe, watch his tragically undersized heart beat on the bedside monitor, sense his struggle and feel the powerful volition that moves him ever forward. I will look at him, and I will feel my own heart move toward his, and I will speak these words:

"Yes. We'll name you *Will*."

Seeing the Course Ahead

Journey

We are, all of us, on a journey through this world, and into the one that we hope waits beyond it. What we'd like, most of us, is a linear path to follow. One with distinct forks in the trail where we could make binary choices to do *right* or *wrong*, or at the very least, to pick between *better* and *worse*. And, as long as we're dreaming, perhaps it could be a temperate path protected from sun and wind, and somehow sheltered from the rain. Oh, and with some nice pavement to keep our feet clean, and with minimal changes in elevation, thank you very much.

But when we're honest with ourselves, we sense that we are instead hiking through a challenging landscape of mixed terrain. Sometimes we press our way through thick brush, or ascend steep rocky paths, or shuffle our feet through hot sand, or weather rainstorms on exposed fields of granite, or hunch our shoulders against the cold. This reality is quite unlike our childhood imaginations of what life would be like, and the unhelpful fantasies that are driven into our brains by mainstream and religious media. No, this thing we call "life" is hard work.

Yet as difficult as it is, the journey is not without reward. Even as we complain about the hardships along the way, we are frequently stopped short by gorgeous vistas and have our breath stolen by moments of rapture. Times when we forget for a moment just how far we've come, and just how far we still have to go. Times when we're filled with joy, and wonder for a second if it is, after all, worth all of the trouble and hardship. Though comprised of both agony and ecstasy, most of the time this monotonous journey consists in our simply putting one foot in front of the other.

We walk because we feel we must, moved ahead by some mandate deep inside us. We walk, though the path—in spite of our earnest wishes to the contrary—is not clear. The Bible that many of us carry turned out to be something other than a step-by-step tour guide with a map for our life in the back. We have a compass too, though its needle wobbles such that we trust it only for gross approximations of direction. And besides, without an orientation to the landscape, a compass is only so helpful. So we squint, trying to discern a faint ribbon of a trail extending before us until we begin to wonder if we're only imagining it. So we look back to see if we've somehow gotten off track, and see a similarly confusing landscape. In our weariness, we realize we couldn't go back if we tried. We can only hope that our effort and intention will count for something, and that we are moving in a good direction.

And yet move we must. Once we've made our choices, we can only look back and wonder if we've done the right thing; if we've been true to ourselves and Whomever we hope is watching over us. And when our choices are made for us—as when my son's heart suddenly stopped—we find ourselves walking in a tumultuous world of flashbacks, memories, celebrations, and doubts. The world of color around us shifts to sepia as the bounce leaves our step and we shuffle forward like walking dead. Indeed, even when we stop and sit down, the landscape continues to come at us in a disorienting mix of fact and imagination, of certainty and doubt. Moving forward requires pulling the levers of our emotional, physical, mental, and volitional resources to see which one will propel us forward on a given day.

From where I sit, typing on a computer just two months after his death, the memories rush at me in a scattered jumble. Some of them are dark caves of doubt, while others are happy recollections of love. Some of them are new and unexpected, while others have become as familiar as the view out the living room window. So that is what follows: the chaotic and nonlinear recollections of a father who has lost his son, who hopes that he hasn't completely lost his way, and who is trying to make sense of it all. I present these thoughts in the same random, non-chronological stream in which they flow through my brain.

Palliative Faith

The intricate surgery that my son experienced at three days of life was called *palliative*—a repair designed to work well enough, and for long enough, to get the patient to the next point in his or her treatment. Palliative repairs are those that come in a series—one repair builds on the one before it and aims to enable the surgery that will follow. Which seems unsatisfying. One might wonder why the surgeons can't just get everything right the first time—until, that is, one recalls the rate of growth in a newborn. Simple things like stitches and scars would heal and grow with the body's structures, of course, but the more necessary artificial implements would not be so simple. If the surgeons attached a Gore-Tex shunt to Will's walnut-sized heart, for example, they would install an intentionally oversized piece that wouldn't actually work well until he grew to a size proportional to the repair. Then, for a matter of days or weeks, the repair would work at optimal efficiency, in fact encouraging the very growth that would make it less effective later on, until it was finally so inefficient that it would need to be replaced.

So our son's heart would need at least three major cardiac surgeries, not including any additional unforeseen repairs or any less invasive cardiac catheterizations. Interspersed with these repairs, we would schedule facial surgeries with a plastic surgeon to repair his cleft lip and palate—a closure of the palate first, then a repair to his upper lip, then final adjustments to both as well as to his nose and surrounding facial structures. So amid the more important palliative cardiac surgeries, our son would also have palliative plastic surgeries, which were likewise prioritized to bring functionality to his facial features before addressing the more cosmetic concerns. In the totality of his treatment, the general plan was to address his problems from largest—i.e., most life-threatening—to smallest.

As difficult as it was to do so, we learned to focus on the current procedure and not be overwhelmed with the whole regimen of two years of surgeries and hospital stays and home care to come. We learned to stave off the guilt of putting him through so much in the short term by noting that his life was threatened by his incapacities. We learned to ignore the waves of guilt related to the subsequent pain and interventions to come by focusing on the long-range good that we hoped would be the result. We learned to let "good enough" be just that, and to be as content as we could be in the moment.

Though many might disagree, I think our faith is palliative, too. Faith needs to work well enough to get us further along, and we are allowed to make adjustments as we go along the journey of life. I know that many would suggest the elements of faith can be mastered—that through proper doctrine or creeds or spiritual laws or comprehensive education we can arrive at a place of confidence and surety, which will allow us clear sailing through the travails of this life and into the next. Maybe I'm just making excuses for failing to master such a faith and for not finding the confidence therein, but I've found that my faith changes as my life moves forward.

The faith that worked for me when I was seven, nestled into an upholstered easy chair with an illustrated Living Bible on a Sunday afternoon, was palliative. I sat there, reflecting on what I'd heard in Sunday school that day, and decided I should ask Jesus to come into my heart so that I wouldn't have to be afraid of death. It was a beautiful moment, and one that I treasure. But I'm glad my faith has changed since then.

There was the faith that carried me through my teenage years—a deterministic understanding that if something happened, God must have willed it. I struggled during those years to understand how the world worked, entertaining long internal debates about whether I should pray for success on my many fishing trips, or whether it was fair for me to thank God for my avoidance of an auto accident when that seemed unkind to the person who was actually in the wrecked car. Looking back, I think I was developing a faith that God embraced, and accepted at face value, even as I struggled toward greater engagement with God and life and the realities all around me, and as I began to develop a view of the world that didn't put me at the very center. This faith was palliative, preparing me for the growth to come.

There was a faith that sustained me in college as I took nightly walks during cold Chicago winters to beg God for a girlfriend who would become a wife. Staring up at the stars, I offered my confident assertions that I would be a great husband, arguing that reason and justice required I be given a wife. This faith was shaped when the answers to my prayers came and I found myself as a new husband to a beautiful and wonderful wife, yet with a fresh and painful awareness of my own brokenness and inability to love her as I had imagined I would.

This growing faith was tweaked and challenged through several years as a pastor, tested as we joined with some friends to start a church on which we eventually performed a kind of organizational euthanasia and were left feeling orphaned and alone, bereft of community. This faith was stretched during a ten-year journey through infertility, moving uncertainly up the ladder of increasingly invasive treatments, until we felt the mixture of absolute joy and panic that comes with the news that you're pregnant . . . with twins!

It was faith that pulled us through the harrowing experience of trying to thwart a miscarriage, of sitting in the worrisome place of a six-month stretch of bed rest. It was faith that sat with us in the silence of those initial ultrasounds when the room was just very, very quiet and the doctors and technicians were visibly nervous, shuttling into and out of the room with forced smiles. It was faith that gave us hope as we plunged headlong into the world of intensive care and surgery and life support and constant monitoring. And today, it is faith that tries to make sense of a life that is all at once painfully absent the life of a precious firstborn son, but also full of the life of his engaging and completely healthy twin sister.

All of which isn't to say that faith is completely individuated, or that it is so subjective as to be meaningless. Just as we entrusted our son to one of the very best cardiac surgeons in the world, we ought to build our faith with the best ideas and the most sensible and sensitive components. But it seems to me a grave mistake to think that these pieces will be permanent, or foundational, or that they will allow us to somehow soar above the harrowing realities of life and death. Just as the surgery that saved my son's life was developed through successes and failures of many other patients just like him, so my faith is built on the necessarily limited viewpoints of my religious teachers (professors, parents, friends, and others) and—God willing—will be reworked and refined by those who come after me. When our very lives are shaken, we may doubt the most basic of convictions and shift the pieces around in our matrix of belief until we find some stability.

Our faith ought not to be a faith that chooses belief over practice, and it shouldn't be selfish or self-interested; it ought to be a faith that works for us, yes, but one that benefits those around us even more than ourselves, and that leads us to the ultimate end to which we're called—a greater capacity to love. If it looks inward, it ought to do so such that it can give outward in ever increasing measure.

Like a writer's drafts, or a backpacker's tent, or a scientist's hypothesis, or a gardener's weeding, or a parent's relationship with a child, our present faith only needs to work for its appointed time and should in fact be flexible, temporary, and transitory. We shape it as best we can and then let it be shaped by God, ourselves, and our community. Maybe faith is only and ever palliative, intended to start us on a journey of eternal collaboration with our Maker. We exert a lifetime of effort at growing and developing our best understanding of God and the world, and at living the kind of lives that tune us in to the music of the Creator and that fulfill God's hopes and dreams for the world. And we trust that God is ahead of us, and all around us, leading us and loving us and preparing us for what is next.

Control

A few days after the funeral, we had a pediatrician's appointment for our daughter, Ella. It felt strange to do something so mundane in the wake of something so titanic, but it seemed somehow important, too. My wife and I talked about it for a couple of minutes before we decided that we'd keep the appointment, mostly because it seemed comforting to maintain some sort of routine. On our way home, we stopped to get new tires on the car, which was even less important. I made passing mention of this tiny errand on my little blog, which was apparently more than a little disconcerting for our friends who read it.

Truth be told, I only heard thirdhand that folks were surprised, but my fertile mind imagined some withering questions. Questions I was asking myself, too. How could we think about such trivial matters right now? How could we occupy our minds with these banalities? Tires? Really?

Well, it seems heartless, I confess. But I ask you, what should we have done? What do you do when your whole life has fallen apart? Your brain is firing fast, but your heart is weary. And so you crave something normal, something familiar, something ordinary. Errands like this make the world seem less hostile. Participating as consumers helps to give hope that life may indeed go on. Finding a taste of normalcy helps to quell the panic that life will never be the same again.

But even more, this kind of project delivers you from the real enemy: home. Why would we want to go home? Why would we want to sit in the silence, to be trapped inside those walls of memory, to feel the foolishness of our former hope, to recall our old happiness? Why would we want to relive the celebrations we'd had, and revisit the doubts we'd harbored but pushed back? Why would we want to sit in that suddenly torturous space when we could be anywhere else?

So without saying so exactly, we tacitly agreed that we'd stop off in a familiar and favorite part of town to leave the car for the couple of hours it would take to install, balance, and align the tires. Oh, and maybe we could go ahead and do the oil change, ahead of schedule. All of which would mean a few hours in which we could sit and eat and walk and window-shop. Time to do nothing, sure. But more than that, it was time to *not* do something: go home.

On a deeper and perhaps more practical level, I would submit that getting new tires is a way to infinitesimally approach an always elusive goal. One that suddenly seemed impossibly distant: control. When something so basic and bedrock as *life* becomes uncertain, it is only natural to search for something solid. It is but a tiny variable in the risky game of life that we all play every day, but it is an inarguable variable nonetheless. New tires mean better grip, which brings more safety, which tips a tiny bit of control our way. We still have a million things to worry about, but we can worry a little less that our car will leave the road. If we get new tires, we are a little less likely to suffer another tragedy. We've trusted fate, we've trusted the odds, we've trusted medicine, and we've trusted God. And we've lost. We've lost everything, or so it seems. So maybe we can trust in the security we can buy. Maybe we can provide a little control for ourselves.

Coffee Maker

A couple of days before the funeral, I was sitting at the kitchen table, keyboard clattering away as I tried to write myself to clarity about some imponderable idea, tried to come to some acceptance of some unavoidable reality, tried to anesthetize myself against some overwhelming pain.

My dear father-in-law walked in with a smile on his face and a package under his arm. He and my mother-in-law had just returned from Target, she with some adorable clothes for her granddaughter, and he with a state-of-the-art coffee maker, which he promptly displayed to me. It had adjustable heat and brew strength, that great feature where you can brew and pour simultaneously, a timer with a cool digital/analog clock face, as well as a nice gold filter basket. Best of all, it brewed twelve cups at a crack. Thus the perfect tool to jump-start all of the assembled family and friends each morning.

I was startled by this act of generosity, and grateful as always for a new toy. And yet I was shocked as I heard my mouth form these words: "Thanks, Dad. That's perfect. And when you go back home after the funeral, you can just take it with you."

Owing to his generous spirit, he wasn't offended by my apparent ungratefulness, but hesitated for just a second before he went on with his day. Still, the next day I forced myself to apologize for my rudeness, though I was at a loss to explain it. "I have no idea why I said that! I'm so sorry. We'll be happy to use the coffee maker, every day."

But the truth is, it's still sitting in the back of a closet.

I think what I was longing for on that confusing morning was to turn back the clock. I was looking for a small, containable, familiar life. I wanted to go back to using our undersized, weathered stainless-steel French press and its familiar routine of heating water, grinding beans, combining the two, stirring the slurry, filling the rest of the pot, putting the lid on, waiting three minutes, and pouring exactly two full cups of coffee—one for me, and one for my wife.

What I didn't want—what I couldn't handle—was a life that was any larger than that. I didn't want any family to be around us. I didn't want houseguests. I didn't want to extend myself in any gesture of hospitality. I wanted to go back to my smaller life of four people—two adults, two tiny children. That smaller life that had been contained by these four walls and its withering 24-hour schedule. If that life had been full to the brim of feedings and medications and baths and tests and interventions and surgeries and home visits and terrifying uncertainty, at least it was familiar and approachable and possible. At least it offered some hope at the end of the day. But this new life I was kicking back against was utterly unfamiliar, dark, and seemingly without hope. It was a life, but it was a life without Will. That old life was a mirage, if it ever really existed. It was gone from my grasp, impossible to reclaim.

I just wanted my old cup of coffee.

Finding a Pace

Heaven

It's hard to say why books that depict heaven as a garden where children run and play all day, never skinning a knee or feeling sad, and who excitedly wait for a reunion with their mother and father, or *Precious Moments* figurines depicting a baby napping on a cloud ("Safe in the Arms of Jesus"), give me the willies.

Why do these expressions bother me? Why are they so offensive to me? Am I just too cynical, or contrary? Why can't I find comfort in these popular views of heaven?

I don't want to insult the nice people who have given these gifts to me. They sincerely intend to encourage me and give us hope and help to heal our broken hearts, and they have done exactly that. They sincerely believe that Jesus cares for little children, and they are surely right.

Still, here is where I stumble over these expressions: these notions presume a static, simplistic view of people and of time. They cement our lost loved ones into fixed roles of how they relate to *me*.

My dearly departed grandfather is exactly that—my father's father. But he was also a brother, a parent, and a friend. Moreover, he was a son, a grandson, and a great-grandson.

So whom, or what, is he now? How old is he in heaven? Which of these many relationships is paramount? Does he have any say over his identity or is it a democracy? Do his more numerous grandchildren get to decide that he will be, say, seventy-four years of age, semiretired, cheerfully mowing the lawns of all our childhood homes, surreptitiously sharing his coffee and Fig Newtons with us, and mischievously making a loud *PFFFT!* sound directly behind us when we'd light firecrackers or engage in some other similarly nerve-wracking project?

Or should he be a rambunctious brother, staging contests to lift the front end of a Model T or shooting .22 caliber bullets into a Salina, Kansas, phone book to see if they penetrate all the way through? Should he be a robust young man with his hair slicked back, yet secretly scared to death of dying, and so making a momentous decision to trust Jesus as his personal Savior? Should he be a handsome, proud, protective bridegroom eagerly anticipating his wedding night? Should he be a father and tenant farmer, demanding that his three young children "get to work!" and yet famously forgiving his preteen son for flipping the family truck into a ditch? Or maybe I'm just selfishly forcing him into categories of *family*. After all, he was a faithful churchman, a devoted friend, and a venerated member of the local community.

After I spoke at his funeral, his close friend came up to commend and amend my eulogy, and I realized there was a whole part of my grandfather's life that—like a small child learning that his parents talk to each other after the kids go to bed—I had completely missed. The man who was my grandfather was a faithful, wholehearted, utterly sincere friend. Which didn't surprise me; it was perfectly congruent with my understanding of him. But the relational lines around my grandfather seemed novel, unfamiliar. Though I knew he had friends, and had in fact talked to this one many times before, I must have thought these friendships were somehow inconsequential or tertiary. Yet here I was, talking with a frail old man who was mourning the loss of a dear friend. "What you said is true," he said as he shook my hand. "Ivar"—I recoiled slightly as I remembered my grandfather had a name other than *Grandpa*—"was exactly the same person in the cornfield on Saturday as he was in church on Sunday."

So who is my son now? Can I even construct the sentence that way? Does he belong to me, or I to him? Or are we instead fellow travelers, each belonging to God? In my yearning to hold him, to kiss him, to buy him cool shoes and watch him learn to walk, to take him fishing, to teach him to pee in the bushes on a hiking trip, or play with him in the surf, am I only holding him back? Hasn't he gone on ahead of me in his journey toward the mountain kingdom? In my constant thinking of him as *my baby boy*, aren't I doing both of us a disservice, torturing myself and forgetting that he was many things to many people, and is right now his own person, quite independent of me?

From whence comes this persistent assumption that in the life hereafter, we will resume these relational connections? Isn't it possible our existence will have greater gravity and purpose than a reunion of family, a recollection of past times, a rehashing of old stories, an eternal reward for services rendered? If the story of God is one of an invitation to people into God's ongoing re-creation and redemption of the world, shouldn't we assume our lives in eternity will be similarly creative and adventurous, rather than an endless lounging on the far side of a pearly finish line? Why, when those in the Bible who were given visions of the hereafter and forced to resort to almost exclusively metaphorical language (streets of gold, mansions with many rooms, jewel-encrusted buildings), do we who have not been so enlightened think we will be able to even imagine what that life might be like?

Why do we assume that we will have familiar, recognizable bodies? In the film *The Matrix*, Neo plugs his brain into a computer-generated world and instantly assumes what his mentor describes as a "residual self-image"—his own perception of himself. At first, he appears as a nervous and unkempt computer hacker in a T-shirt and black canvas jacket. But as his training continues and his confidence grows, his hair gets slicked back, his darting eyes disappear behind dark sunglasses, his jacket turns to leather and lengthens to the floor, and his stance changes from *uncertain* to *supremely confident*. So, which me will I be? Do I have any say over it at all? Will my family or friends determine it, or will God decide? And on what basis? Or are all of these questions misguided?

My sneaking suspicion is that our souls somehow stand apart from such concerns of identity and relationship. Our obsession with riches and rest and comfortable relationships has more to do with our cultural context than with a biblical notion of heaven. Now, inasmuch as *relationship* is such a powerful theme of the story of God—Genesis 1 begins with the Creator in relationship and yearning for more relationship: "Let *us* make mankind in *our* image, in *our* likeness . . ." (emphasis mine)—I'm sure the ever-after will be anything but individualistic. And the value God places on our bodies—Genesis again: God creates human bodies and pronounces them "good"—would suggest that eternity will not be some completely ethereal experience of disembodied souls floating around.

But in my longing and love for my son, I pray that my imagination of what eternal life (his, and mine) might look like is not stunted. I want to release my mental, physical, and spiritual imaginings of him and allow him to lead me into a greater life in God.

Split Personality

What do we do when we're done with what we need to do? Sometime between the funeral and the completion of our grief, we'll need to, for financial or practical reasons, get back to our regular life. After a few days or weeks of empty space, the void becomes overwhelming and we want to make some effort to get back to some semblance of "normal." Yet in moving forward, and in my reengagement with life, I hope I'm not being duplicitous. I hope I'm not projecting a false image of myself or pretending I'm more adjusted and "normal" than I really am. I hope I'm just trying to feed my better self, to foster a more normal relationship with the world around me.

So I tentatively enter back into the life of my primary community, a small church full of religious refugees. A month or so after The Night, I find myself sitting in front of our small Sunday morning assemblage, leading a discussion about prayer. Trying to help our overly analytical group get past its intellectual objections and actually get to gut level and engage with prayer. To stop *talking about* prayer and begin *participating in* prayer. But we've got questions, you see. Good questions: "Why does God ask us to pray, if God already knows everything? Why should we repeat ourselves, since God has perfect hearing and a perfect memory? Is prayer meant to just change us, such that our entreaties to the Almighty are illusory?"

As I sit on my stool at the front of the room, my main objective is to listen, identify with the person speaking, and empathize. I tend to do this fairly well, largely because I recognize that such conversation is genuine—people have lots of baggage, for lots of reasons. "Reactivity" is what we sometimes call this effect of our past imposing itself into our present. We've been subjected to prayer power plays by overeager pastors, survived seasons of unanswered prayer, felt nagging doubts that linger for years, seen our substantial prayers ignored while our friends trip into all kinds of blessings, and found general frustration with the process of prayer. And we are all in various stages of engagement with doing something about our bad pasts, with cutting ourselves free from the entanglements of our history. So I listen to these people whom I love, and feel for them, and identify with everyone's objections and concerns.

Then I sum up, conclude our discussion time, step off my stool, and sit down as we move toward a time of Eucharist. And just as my physical viewpoint shifts, so does my mental perspective. From here, I feel a little blood rush back into my chest and remember my own pain, disappointment, frustration, anger. Unfortunately, it gets directed back against my friends, as I give an imaginary and sarcastic speech to them:

You think you have intellectual difficulty with prayer? Do you wonder how it works? Wow, that must be *so* difficult! Have you ever prayed that your child would be healed in utero? Have you ever prayed until you can't anymore, or maybe you come to a place where your very thoughts and desires are themselves prayer—where you've either given up on prayer entirely or entered into it so deeply that actually forming words or thoughts is irrelevant? Have you ever asked God for answers about how best to care for your child and heard mostly silence? Have you sat by his bed, day after day, unable to even pray for his needs because you know that God knows them anyway, and doesn't seem too interested in helping? Or felt the heartbreaking agony of having prayers for healing answered by an even longer list of physical maladies? Have you ever prayed that your son would come off a ventilator and gotten your answer in a paralyzed diaphragm? Have you ever stood in the hallway, praying your son's heart starts again, only to see the doctor approach you without actually looking you in the eye? Have you ever washed his clothes for the last time, deeply disappointed that they've lost their distinctive odor and just smell like all the other dirty laundry? Have you ever given a huge box of his diapers away, or taken his crib apart and put it in the closet because you couldn't stand to look at it anymore? Have you ever bought a tiny casket in a rush of preparation before a rapidly approaching funeral and wondered if you should pray or curse when it isn't delivered on time?

I listen to myself rant at my loving friends, and I wonder if I'm pretending—afraid that I'm a sham who is feigning composure. My hope is that the listening, giving, leading *me* sitting on the stool is a more real version of me, the me I used to be and the me I'll become again, someday. I feel like I'm trying to get "back" to something, and I find my way to the neighborhood, only someone has switched all the street signs and there's a parking lot where my house used to be. What do I do in the meantime, and what if I can't ever get back? How can I help them, and myself, get to where we all want to go?

So I gather up my two selves, wipe my eyes, stand, and walk forward to partake of the Eucharist.

Eulogy

One of the great sadnesses and deep regrets of this week is that more of you couldn't have known my son. His life had many limitations that prevented him from spending time with many people. Moreover, his parents had limitations that kept us to ourselves. Between medical appointments, in-home care, therapies, feedings, meetings, and naps, it was hard for many of you to get to know him, or even meet him. For better and worse, Stacy and I knew him better than anyone. For this, I am both deeply regretful and oddly impenitent. So today I wanted to tell you about William Addison Stavlund.

First, you need to know that he was stinky. Between his heavy workload, his high metabolism, his constant sweating, his persistent eye infection, his regular reflux, his many meds, those wretched liquid vitamins with iron, and his distaste for baths, he was usually pretty gamey. But I loved that stinky boy. No matter how short or noisy the night, I'd always take him out of his bed in the morning, feel his clammy clothes, and nuzzle my face to his shoulder. Even when I'd gag a little at the stench, I'd still say, "Mmmm . . . oh, I love my stinky boy!"

And he was stubborn. If he was unhappy, he'd let you know. His cardiologist told us to never feed him or stress him for more than twenty to thirty minutes, but she forgot to tell him. He'd scream and cry for twice that long if he felt like it. If you held him up to try to get him to stand, his legs would go completely floppy. But if you tried to change or feed him, he might kick you the whole time. To give him a bottle was to try to hit a moving target, as he twisted and turned his head in frequent noncooperation. And if you did get the nipple into his mouth, he could clamp down on it so hard that you couldn't pull it out.

And he was beautiful. His little sister might have been bigger, but he was graced with gorgeous features. His eyelashes were long and luscious, and his downy hair would shine red, brown, or blond, depending on the light. Oh, and those eyes. The deepest blue, they would draw you in and make you forget absolutely everything. They were such a spectacle that otherwise responsible nurses and techs would be sorely tempted to wake him up, or at least to stick their faces in front of his to steal that gaze. So persistent was this problem that one of the cardiac ICU nurses finally threw a sheet over his crib to make a tent and then put up a Do Not Disturb sign. Which everyone promptly ignored.

He was determined. With Will, everything was an effort, yet he would tirelessly chip away at the mountain in front of him. If he ran into something overwhelming, he would pause to catch his breath and then just keep pushing ahead. I've run the Boston Marathon twice, but I've never seen anyone work so hard. At times, it was honestly difficult to watch. Day and night, hour by hour, minute by minute. Against impossible impediments: half of a heart, a partially paralyzed diaphragm, a shrinking aorta, a cleft lip and palate, low birth weight, digestive problems, and oral aversions, he pushed and pushed and pushed. He was the strongest person I've ever known.

He was full of hope. His life stood as a beacon of hope, an example of what it means to walk by faith and not by sight. When our hope flagged, he defied our expectations. When tests and X-rays and reports came back ominous, he cruised ahead. When we worried, he paid no attention. He fooled us all. He was strong when he was supposed to be weak, and—in the end—he was weak when we thought he would be strong.

And he was wise. I know I shouldn't say this about a baby, but I can't help it. To look into his eyes was to be lost in a bottomless pool. It seemed that you could see into his very soul. Or perhaps he saw into your soul. Either way, the journey was revealing, and a little disconcerting. I would constantly wonder if there was much, much more that he knew, and we eagerly awaited the day when he could share that with us. He was a tiny baby, yes, but he was also a real person—flesh, soul, and spirit.

Now he's gone, and we're angry and empty and lost.

I wonder:

Maybe this searing pain is what it feels like to be touched by love.

Maybe this searing pain is what it feels like to be touched by God.

Maybe we've seen and watched and touched something that will change us.

Many years ago, a friend prayed and prophesied that my wife would have a daughter and a son, and that the boy would bring God's kingdom. That he would, in some small way, usher in this realm where, as Jesus described, God's will is done, on earth as it is in heaven. Six years later, we held Ella and Will, and we began to see the truth of this. He drew goodness and grace out of us, and others. We hoped that he would continue to do so as a marathoner, as one who completes a long and arduous course. Today, we are greatly grieved to realize he was instead a relay runner, who has passed the baton to us who gather here today. We who knew him from near and far touched, tasted, and felt the kingdom that Jesus spoke of and lived in. It is left to us to carry that baton, to live full of love and without reserve, and to stay strong until the end as God gives us strength.

Good-bye, William Addison Stavlund. We will love you and remember you. We thank you, and we thank God for you. Amen, and amen.

Catching My Breath

Clothes Horse

I'm just going to go ahead and say it: I'm kind of a clothes horse. I treasure my clothes, whether they be fancy or functional.

Even now, when I close my eyes, I can still see my first pair of jeans. Well, the first ones I got that weren't Sears Toughskins, anyway. Moved to compassion by my awkward entry into a new school in the eighth grade, my mother took me to Lindale Mall in Cedar Rapids, Iowa, where I strode haltingly into a bright store called The Buckle and tried to act like that woman with me wasn't my mom but just someone I knew. There, my eyes riveted on them—jeans that weren't blue, but bleached almost white. They weren't stacked on a shelf, segregated according to size—oh no!—they were clipped to a hanger on a circular rack. My hands stroked the soft fabric and found their way to a plasticized tag stitched onto the watch pocket. White letters over a red background read *Unionbay: Wears Like a Pig's Nose*. This seemed like a stirring and powerful metaphor, but one that was a tad agrarian for designer jeans. Even as I wondered about the juxtaposition, I realized my new modus—cool—would require a kind of imperviousness to such trivialities. I waited as my mother paid for the pants, then stepped out of the store and into my new life.

When I was attending college near Chicago, my friends and I would regularly pile into a car to visit the many thrift stores in the city. Village Thrift was the most impressive: stuffy and hot no matter the season, it often reeked of body odor and pungent food, but could be counted on to deliver the most amazing and affordable treasures. My buddies and I would bust through the door with the urgent awareness that, though best of friends, we were now competing with one another for the best and cheapest prizes. Looking back, I see that we tended to segregate according to course of study. Business and marketing people would speed-walk to check on suits, white oxford shirts, and dress shoes. Finding anything of quality in this section was a bit unsettling, as we would imagine that only death would separate a man from a pristine pair of wing tips or a five-hundred-dollar suit. But no matter, at five bucks apiece, my econ-minded friends were buying now and asking questions later.

Information technology majors would scroll through the khaki pants and polos, while students of the hard sciences would search out the T-shirts and jeans. Most disturbingly, one of my friends would fearlessly venture over to buy any pair of boxer shorts that fit him. This was anathema to even otherwise hardcore thrifters (and especially anyone who had taken microbiology), but he was confident that a good washing would render them harmless. He was an English major who graduated from a respected law school and went on to become a successful attorney. He currently represents a major appliance manufacturer, and so I suspect his expectations of laundry equipment are much more reasonable now.

But Bible students like me were countercultural and unconcerned with such social conventions. We flew through the flannel shirts, looking for something to wear over our old T-shirts. We knew how to efficiently assess hundreds in a matter of minutes: push and pull an empty gap into the long rack, then flip through each shirt. Hearing the *shik shik shik* of the sliding hangers was hypnotic, so you had to concentrate to pick out any label or pattern that might interest you. Then a quick check for holes and missing buttons, and the keepers would get flung across your shoulder. At forty or ninety cents apiece, we could throw a sizeable pile of flannel shirts on the counter and get most of a ten back. So, yes, I must have been quite a sight as I weathered those Chicago winters: I simply added another shirt for every five-degree drop in temperature, until the lapels stacked up and made it hard to turn my head. I was like Joseph in my multicolored coat of many collars.

Even now, with a long-suffering wife to thwart my bad fashion impulses and push back my embarrassing nostalgia, I've got a nice little collection of clothes. Small, but it's precious to me. When I stand in front of it, I think about how I'm feeling that day, what I'll do and who I'll see, and I pick out something that will present my true self to the world.

For the first two months of Will's life, we would go to the hospital. Every single day. To see him, of course, and to spend time with his twin sister and whichever family members might be with us or whichever friends might be stopping by. But also to interact with the nurses, talk with the techs, and meet with the doctors. So my expression of myself was always tempered. I wanted people to know the real me, but I also wanted to let them know I was upright and respectable. Casual, maybe, but sober about the work ahead of us. I knew I didn't want to get caught conferring with a world-class cardiologist about some grave condition while she glanced at my frayed collar.

On one memorable day, I forgot to pack a spare, and my dear Ella decorated the front of my shirt with feces. One of the nurses kindly grabbed me an extra T-shirt out of the stash intended for vagrant parents, and I spent the rest of the day hoping I wouldn't meet anyone new, lest they think that I was the kind of person who would wear a wrinkly white T-shirt with garish printing on it to my child's bedside.

When we went back to the hospital for a diagnostic evaluation, I put together a kit of clothes for a couple of days, a blend of comfort and fashion that would allow me to sleep on couches and still look decent. On that day I wore a short-sleeved, black button-down shirt, plain jeans, black leather shoes with round toes, and carried a backpack with some other shirts and pants and underwear and socks. At the last minute I remembered I needed to have something to wear overnight. This is not a huge segment of my wardrobe, as I mysteriously associate pajamas with the constraints of childhood. Fortunately, after suffering through too many Christmas mornings with me shuffling around in bare feet and the clothes I wore the night before, my dear in-laws have made regular gifts of pajamas and slippers. Hint taken.

So on that dark night, that Black Tuesday, I found myself pacing the halls in my flannel pajama bottoms and a gray T-shirt bearing the logo of my brother's carpentry business. Even in the chaos of those moments, I felt proud to wear my family name at a time like this. I thought about my father and grandfather and great-grandfather, who had worried over their own sons. I didn't feel quite so alone. Looking down as I moved and muttered to myself, trying not to cry or scream or pass out, I noticed something else. On my feet were my very favorite shoes: brown flip-flop sandals that had carried me to beaches in Mexico and Costa Rica, had eased the burning of my soles as I hobbled to the car after two separate marathons, as well as moved me through supermarkets and big-box stores in suburban Virginia. This seemed right and familiar, shoes that had lived my life with me and were accordingly weathered. But the whole package—T-shirt, flannel pajama pants, and broken-down sandals—seemed a little embarrassing when I looked at the throng of people who were pretending not to stare at me.

I came to myself a bit after everyone left the bedside. I picked up his body and held him close. I remembered that my wife was on her way in, and that people would be coming, and besides, it just isn't right at a time like this to wear a T-shirt and flannel pants and flip-flops. So I set him down, tugged the curtain closed, and changed back into the clothes I had been wearing just a couple of hours before. I was glad to be able to put on a black shirt, to show by my exterior what I felt in my interior.

In the days that followed, I kept reaching for more black shirts, until I felt myself gravitating to the discount men's clothing store up the hill from our house. By then, my brother-in-law was with us and he accompanied me on what must have looked like a mission of madness. I was a little self-conscious of my sudden consumerism, yet at some visceral level I needed more black T-shirts, and I needed new black shoes. Tim helped me pick out the new shoes. He suggested a pair with squarer toes, and I liked them immediately. In my mind I thought I was looking for something newer, fresher, more worthy of the occasion of the memorial service at our home. But I would later think about my disinclination to wear my normal black shoes, and would realize it was more than propriety or fashion. It was that they were the shoes I wore *that night* as I gave my wife the unspeakable news. It wasn't that I was rejecting their worn edges and round toes; I was simply refusing to walk in those shoes again.

On that first trip for black T-shirts and shoes, I tried on a few black dress shirts, too. I was halfheartedly looking for one to wear to the funeral, and not having much success. Finally, after searching through a dozen, I found one that was nice but a little more expensive than I thought it should be:

it was twenty-five bucks instead of twenty. So I shrugged it off. Several days later, pushing back panic, I was in the store again, brother-in-law at my side, looking for that same shirt. Unfortunately, that same shirt was gone.

I tried to be calm, to act as if I didn't really mind. Like I was just as happy to wear my black suit and black tie, with black shoes and a white shirt. The same thing I've worn to every other funeral I've attended. But I wasn't, and didn't have any more time to do anything about it. I wouldn't be able to present my most honest self, clad entirely in black, to those gathered at the funeral.

I still needed to buy handkerchiefs for the funeral, plus black socks and black boxer shorts. We stood in line at the register, making small talk and watching the guy in front of us, who was buying a suit by peeling several hundred-dollar bills from a huge stack. As we left the store and I drove Tim to the Metro, I woke up to reality. It was a Saturday night, and his friends had been cooking most of the day in anticipation of a low-key get-together with him as honored guest. Only my silly shirt boondoggle had made him miss most of it. Chagrined, I apologized for keeping him from his friends and his food. I told him how embarrassed I was to waste his time looking for nonexistent shirts. About how silly I felt to have him see me like this, dependent and adrift all at the same time. But he understood that this wasn't about clothes, not at all.

"No," he said. "These are the things that matter."

Community

It is passé to say that "people wear masks." It's a tired caricature, and one so obviously true as to be senseless. Moreover, such a broad-brush critique is silly, for this phenomenon is in fact commendable. After all, where would we be without personas? What would the world look like if each of us shared everything about ourselves to every person we ever met? The economics alone would be staggering—we'd be spending almost unlimited time vomiting up our entire personal histories and all our dark secrets to people at the gas station, on the commuter train, and in the checkout line. Who needs that? What would be the benefit? How would we get anything done?

The other extreme, however, is not any better. It is one we know all too well: fragmented lives lived in the midst of disjointed relationships. In twenty-first century North American culture, most people live in a kind of self-imposed solitary confinement. Many of us live in families, yes, but we aspire to house them in large buildings parceled out into many rooms, which sit on sizeable pieces of land. We have personal computers, personal music players, personal meals, and enough televisions that we don't need to compromise on which program we'd like to see. We can become so isolated in our little worlds that we may only be visible to our neighbors when we're behind the wheel of our vehicles, hurrying off to make more money to pay for it all. And for those of us in more urban environments, things aren't much different. We may live in smaller spaces, and in closer proximity to one another, but this seems to only increase the psychic space we put between ourselves and our neighbors. Go to a coffee shop and you'll see three strangers sharing a table, laptops open, and nary a word spoken between them. Walk down a city street and you'll be lucky if one person returns your gaze. Say hello or wave and you'll likely be stared at as the freak that you are.

These observations are not meant as critique—not exactly. Psychic space is a good thing, a healthy thing, a normalizing force for good. It's a fair compromise for us, creatures with limited social energy. And yet, when our lives are full of pain, we often feel utterly alone. Quite ironic, since most of the people we see are in pain as well. If not right now, then in the recent past. If not in the recent past, then in the near future. We are alone, and we are not alone, trapped on parallel lines that we fear will never converge.

When our son was first diagnosed in utero, and my faith was stretched and my hope was eroded, I reflected on this experience of pain, and this feeling of alienation, in a poem.

Caught in the Middle

searching for emotion
that eludes me
but somehow
sneaks up behind with a tap on the shoulder
torrents of inopportunity

it is just below the surface
somehow
deep and overwhelming
I could drown in it, I know
yet it is silent and still
at least for now

prone to sadness and self-pity
I've been much more worked up
over a lot less
so this is eerie
eerily calm.

I want to be angry,
sad, disappointed,
forlorn, depressed
but I'm just
. . . nothing

I walk slowly through the store,
wondering why everyone is staring at me
until I realize
I'm on my fourth lap

of the produce section
and haven't touched anything

I'm the one who is looking at them
taking in their faces
looking into their eyes
in the way that people
don't

Looking for something
some sign of recognition or pain
some signal that they feel something
that they know something
that they have come through suffering intact
that I'm not alone

the empty
is inside of me
waiting for the other shoe
to drop
so that I can explode

but I don't want to explode
or even simmer
I want to walk smoothly
through the fire
and come out on the other side
"though he slay me, yet will I trust him"

stuck inside my head
analytical about emotion
chasing the tail of the dog
that might soon turn on me

Moving in the artificial light
of an ongoing day
the hands of the clock
turn late into the night
but they do not beckon me

I sleep lightly
and wake up to another day
not sleepy or rested
not anxious or invigorated

just moving through the landscape
of people whose lives continue on
surely they have sadness
heartbreak, tragedy

Everyone takes their turn at this
don't they?
everyone goes through their fire
everyone wonders wearily

If it is our collective story
then we never tell it
never reveal it
never

All of us have felt utterly alone, haven't we? Some have suffered more than others, but we've all come to a place where we doubt that we can go on. We've all wondered if there is any force of love and logic behind everything (some have decided there isn't, and I don't blame them one bit). We may not have all had the courage to act on our feelings, but haven't we all thought that the end of our lives wouldn't be so bad, after all? Or at least admitted that the end would be easier than continuing to plod along the path?

We've all felt this, or we all feel this, but we don't acknowledge it. We keep our pain to ourselves. We keep our struggles private and pretend things aren't so bad.

Ironically, this seems to be especially true in many communities of faith, where the high value placed on noble ideas like *faith* and *hope* and *higher power* and *redemption* can work to quell voices to the contrary, and can lead to the denial of the basic human condition. Like eavesdropping on one side of a telephone conversation, or reading every other page of a book, we learn only half of the story. Surely, things like faith, hope, love and salvation are good. They are, in my view, the answers we long for, and which we desperately need. But the answers are not enough—we need the questions. For what is salvation without alienation? What is redemption without loss? What is hope without despair? What is love without betrayal? If we pretend that those who experience despair, betrayal, alienation and pain are only those outside our communities of faith, then we deprive ourselves of honestly facing our own brokenness, and connecting with one another and with God. We pretend that we have risen above the heartbreaks and ambiguities that are a part of the human condition.

Recently a few of us in our church got together over the course of several Sunday evenings to tell the story of our lives. To try to find the plotline of our experiences: the dreams and aspirations we suspect God is trying to enact through our lives. It was a wonderful, hope-filled time of connection. And yet, as we circled around the living room, we heard person after person talk about difficulty, disappointment, and depression. About how significant chapters of their stories were times when they felt utterly alone. Although, in this room of honesty and with the benefit of hindsight, we all realized we were not alone. We may have been isolated, but we weren't alone. And it cannot be the case that we who had felt such alienation just happened to assemble in this living room for these gatherings. Surely, the people who were the participants in our stories—our friends, family, co-workers, and community members—had been suffering, too. But somehow they didn't, or wouldn't, know about our struggles. And we didn't, or wouldn't, know about theirs. We set ourselves on parallel tracks and moved ahead, alone in our community of pain. Alone, and not alone.

It is tempting, when we experience this false sense of isolation, to plunge ahead, ignoring social constructs and personal boundaries. We taste the comforts of real community and we crave even more. Often we're tempted to force something to happen, in spite of ourselves and the people with whom we'd like to connect.

Even in the midst of our difficulties, my wife and I have chafed at these limitations of social convention. We long to extend our true selves to our neighbors, to our friends, and even to the nameless people we encounter. But how to change things? Too often we reach out to others in clumsy and desperate ways, our own worst enemies. We blurt things out, unkindly inflicting our pain and despair on others.

On a couple of occasions we've even opened up to cab drivers during rides to the airport. After offering a greeting and throwing our circus-sized menagerie of bags into the trunk, we'll set to the serious work of strapping the car seat into the middle of the back seat and belting ourselves in. Once under way, when the cab driver has commented on the cuteness of the baby and cheerfully inquired about other children we might have, one of us will unabashedly lay it all out: "Well, our daughter had a twin, but he died recently." It is a kind of hopeful, if admittedly brutal, test of social conventions. We wonder if our fellow humans will accept our honesty and perhaps reciprocate about some loss or deficit or brokenness in their lives. So far we're batting .500. We've gotten one subdued and shocked acknowledgment, and one long-winded sales pitch for a life-insurance pyramid scheme. I'm not sure if that is a sign of hope or hopelessness, but I'm pretty sure we've been blacklisted by our cab company.

So how do we get connected? How can we move from parallel motion to face-to-face sharing? How do we cross the threshold of humanity and just be honest? How can we leave our lives of isolation to find community?

Well, I don't know, exactly. It is dangerous work, to be sure. Say too much, or say it too soon, and your potential partner in pain will recoil in shock. If you are too honest, they will run away, or, worse yet, they will stay to set up camp in an attempt to bandage over your painful parts with platitudes too unbearable to repeat here. But try and fail a few times, and work hard to find the right person, and you will see the face of God. You will see eyes bordered by tears looking back at you, a wordless message that says, *I feel your pain, and I share it with you.* And then they will open themselves up to you too, because they will know that you understand.

Leg Cramps

Funeral Home

The cell phone lit up with a number that seemed vaguely familiar, but which I couldn't quite place. "Good afternoon, Mr. Stavlund. This is Wayne, from the funeral home. I'm at the crematory."

It is times like these that I hate euphemisms with all of their imprecision. What did he mean exactly? Was he just pulling up to the industrial park where the crematory was located? Did I have time to drive there myself, as I had half hoped? Could I help carry the casket and his body inside? Is there a place where I can sit and wait? Or is everything already under way—has the metal curtain come down and the burner been fired? In which case, can I make it there in time to watch the smoke? Do I really want to?

And so it was that a few days after we said good-bye to him, the beloved body of my dear son was consumed in flames. The decision that his mother and I made about what to do with his earthly body was a lonely and crushing one. It was something we had decided many months before, as we explored all the dark possibilities of loss of pregnancy, and stillbirth, and his not surviving surgery, and many other potentialities.

Before they were even born, we decided we would have the bodies of our children cremated in the event of their death.

All of which went right out the window on that Black Tuesday. Once we had known and loved his body, and once we saw him struggle so mightily through and against it, and once we held that precious flesh after his life had departed it, we were at a complete loss to remember why we would ever choose cremation. It seemed like such a disrespectful thing to do—to destroy this beautiful vessel, and to grind up the remaining bits of bone. It seemed brutal and manifestly unkind. But was burial any better? Is a long process better than a quick one? We doubted it, especially several days later when we met with the funeral director and looked at catalogs of caskets. Epoxies, polyurethanes, vaults, and hermetic seals seemed more than a little illusory as they arrested and then expanded the process of decomposition. In the end, hard as it was, we decided to choose an all-wood casket and cremation.

This turned out to be an unexpectedly challenging proposition. Not that the folks at the funeral home weren't exceedingly helpful—everyone was kind and quiet and composed and deliberate and friendly, in the manner of such people in such places. They were compassionate and personable, even. They took their time in listening to us tell our story, and shared their own stories, too.

So we found ourselves sitting across a round table from a plainspoken man wearing a white shirt and flowered tie, with several catalogs of unappealing pressed-wood and faux felt-covered caskets scattered between us. "Yeah," he said, gesturing to the literature. "These won't do. You don't want some fake wood. You want something real and solid and beautiful for your son. I'm surprised we don't have something like that available. But I'll tell you what—and I know it sounds strange, but I used to work there—I know they have nicer caskets than these at the pet cemetery. I'll call over there in the morning."

Unsure of the outcome of such an endeavor, and at a loss for what we'd tell our family when asked, "Where did you find such a beautiful casket?" we did something so common that it seems sacrilegious. After returning home, we gathered our assembled extended family to fire up a couple of laptops and do Google searches on the World Wide Web.

Casket baby wood was a startling phrase to see in the search window. Almost like a reminder that this had, in fact, happened. But we didn't have time to dwell on that now. We quickly spoke our findings out in a kind of stream-of-consciousness attempt to avoid duplicating any of our efforts. The clock was ticking; it was Thursday night, and the funeral was Monday afternoon. Finally, someone found a Trappist casket company. A group of Catholic monks in Indiana run a publishing house and a casket shop. Their life-work—their religious service—is providing prayer-soaked, arrestingly beautiful wooden caskets for families in need. My wife dialed the number, inquired about any very small caskets they might have in stock, made some scratchings on a pad of paper, said "Thank you," and closed her cell phone. So we had a solid option, even as we continued our World-Wide search.

After much more searching, we agreed that this was a great casket (and at a fair price), so I called back, credit card in hand. We agreed on terms and quickly chose the most expeditious shipping option, even as the woman speaking to me loaded the package in her car and raced off to the shipping center. She was confident we'd have it by Friday, and I breathed a huge sigh of relief.

She called to follow up the next day, leaving a voice mail on my wife's phone. Apparently, she had missed the pickup by mere minutes, but not to worry. The casket would easily arrive by Monday. *Monday?* My wife spared me the aggravating update and simply returned the call. She kindly informed the woman that *the funeral* was Monday and asked if there was any way the delivery could be expedited for Saturday. With understanding and apology, our casket contact confirmed that this would be taken care of. We'd have the package by noon on Saturday.

So I busied myself on Saturday morning, tidying up the house and doing some writing. Almost as if on cue, I ascended out of my escapism at five minutes after twelve, opened up a Web browser, and tried to check on the status of my package. It was then I realized that, owing to our phone transaction, I didn't have a tracking number for the casket. So I searched for the telephone number of the casket company, dialed it, and didn't find anyone who might help me there. As I walked out the door and around to the front of the house, I was already dialing the number for customer service at the shipping company.

The first response to my query, "I'm sorry, sir, but we can't track a package without a tracking number," was what I'd expected. I explained the entire situation again and implored the person to make whatever exception was necessary. When that was ineffectual, I breathed deeply (yet quietly) and asked to speak to a supervisor.

I kept myself mostly composed when I was speaking with people, but when placed on hold I screamed obscenities into the air. Where was the package? What would we do without it? How could they tell me there was nothing they could do when surely there was someone, somewhere, who could locate the package by using my name and delivery address? I needed to know where it was so I could retrieve it. I needed to know where it was so we could carry my son in it in forty-eight hours. I needed to know where it was so I could *do something*—something besides pacing back and forth, ranting into a cell phone. Finally, with no help forthcoming, I gave up the goal and ended the call.

Returning to our kitchen, I happened to glance out the window as a large brown truck rolled down the street. Without a second glance I dashed out the door, rounded the corner to the driveway, and to my consternation found it to be inexplicably empty!

And so it was that at 12:40 p.m. on a sunny Saturday afternoon, I found myself jogging up the street in the direction I had last seen the truck heading. After a few hundred yards, I heard the familiar sound and saw the truck cresting the hill toward me. The driver stopped to say he'd be "right there." I breathed deeply and thanked him, even as I turned around and wondered how he knew who I was and what I was looking for. As I came to myself, the answer was all too clear. Who else but a grieving father would be so disheveled and obviously distraught, wearing shorts, a T-shirt and flip-flop sandals, running up the hilly residential streets with a cell phone in his hand?

The driver was almost priestly as he apologized for his delay, and as he wordlessly carried the large cardboard box off the truck. He even took pains to make sure the box remained level and upright. His words were few, and his eyes were moist. "I'm sorry" was all he said as he obviously understood what it meant for such an anxious and fearful man to receive such a small package from a casket company. I cradled the box in my arms and gently lowered it to the driveway, utterly exhausted.

After a day and night of sitting with this work of art, this gift to our son's memory, we finally boxed it back up and delivered it to the funeral home on Sunday afternoon. While there, we also intended to view and perhaps dress the body of our son. I look back now and cringe. Not because of any audacity on our part—I'm glad we were bold enough to satisfy our sincere curiosity and see what his body looked like. I'm glad we overcame our fear and faced the sight of his pale body, wrapped in a blanket and held in a wicker basket.

I'm glad for the opportunity to look at him and say, out loud, "There's no life in his body anymore. He's really gone."

I don't cringe because of the businesslike demeanor—even sterile professionalism—of the kind man who shepherded us through that hour, who greeted us at the door, and led us down the hall, and opened the double doors, and followed us in, and then stepped back the perfect distance to answer any question or fulfill any request. He stood there in his black suit and averted his eyes in a silent vigil.

"Can we fix his hair?" we asked. "He has such beautiful hair, and he usually wore it a little mussed up, but it's all plastered with hair spray now." "Yes, of course," he said, and graciously excused himself to reappear several minutes later bearing shampoo, a towel, sterile gloves, and more hair product.

No, I don't cringe because we went there that day. I don't cringe because we went and touched his body and saw where they had made incisions for the embalming, then sewed them shut with white string. I cringe because I fear that an unquestioned, bedrock assumption I made that day might have been utter foolishness. Downstairs, in the brightly lit room where the bodies are prepared, I take it as a given that his body was not viewed with derision. I'm completely confident that the people there were caring, nurturing even. I'm sure they felt sadness, and moved with reverence and compassion as they completed their work of embalming and preparing.

No, I cringe because, looking back, it is painful to think that my son might have been seen even with objectivity. That he would be looked upon with something other than overwhelming love. For the situation is not as it would seem. His was not a fatally flawed body that marked time until its faculties failed. He was not some lost cause who was just waiting to die. He was not broken. He was an exceedingly strong person who found the grace to miraculously triumph over his body and all of its limitations. He was complete and whole and glorious and utterly beloved.

Maybe that's the real purpose of all of these funerary rites: in many ways, from multiple angles, to face the reality of our loss and the limits of our powers, and to accept that other people's perceptions are not in our control. To learn how to, in the words I read from a fortune cookie a few months later, *Accept something that you cannot change, and you will feel better.*

Remembering Rightly

One of my favorite theologians is Miroslav Volf, whose multi-layered work betrays a bright intellect and a broad interest in psychology, sociology, literature, and all that it means to be human. I've recently read *The End of Memory*. While it's primarily about dealing with the offenses we've each suffered from others—about remembering these things accurately and in finding a way to suspend vengeance and find the path to forgiveness—his thoughts are spurring mine.

These days, there's a tendency to contort my memories of my son to reinforce my general sense of things, to read the end into the beginning and middle of the story so that all my memories become tainted with my current feelings of sadness, regret, and guilt. In Volf's terms, I see myself as both the victim and perpetrator of something terrible, and so condemn myself for not doing or seeing or being more for him.

Even when I'm remembering some happy occasion—a laugh, a large bottle, a happy bath, or a walk outside—I bend it to focus on a negative aspect of the event, or the foreshadowing of trouble that I see in retrospect, or the fleeting nature of the pleasures. Or failing that, I take the whole memory and bemoan the fact we didn't take more walks or baths or photos or whatever.

One of our more enjoyable afternoons found us sitting beside the pool on the property where we live. The day was sunny, the air temperate, and, due in no small part to my uber-competent sister who was visiting for the week, we were uncharacteristically motivated to set up the portable oxygen and go to the trouble of carrying that tank and the pulse-oxygen monitor the sixty or so steps from our apartment to the pool. We even carried a bottle of milk and, after showing Will around a bit, sat down to a late lunch while his sister kicked her feet in the water. It was simple, beautiful, triumphant, and I treasure the photos we took that day.

"Lunch alfresco" is our shorthand for it now. I smile when I think of it. I'm deeply thankful for those thirty minutes, and so I refuse to let that memory be tainted by any other thought.

It was a great day. Nothing more, and nothing less.

Sparrows

In the middle of our winter of waiting, when we were watching my wife's belly grow by the day, and when we were using ultrasound to check on the babies every week, a large flat package showed up at our house. It wasn't heavy, and its return address didn't ring any bells.

I started opening it up and for several minutes worked my way through alternating layers of paper and cardboard, until I noticed a wooden corner wrapped in canvas and realized it was a painting. Two paintings actually. Our friends had been traveling around the country in their car, making a large canvas a serious logistical problem. So they teamed up to make a diptych, a single work on two canvases.

The background is a rich, almost random collection of muted colors and textures—small swaths of color tooled onto the surface. A spindly, multiforked branch extends across the entire width of both canvases, and on the branch, five tiny birds are randomly spaced. At the bottom right is this simple inscription in pencil: *"Aren't five sparrows worth about two cents? And yet not one of them is forgotten in your Father's sight."* The words of Jesus, taken from the gospel of Luke.

Holding the two pieces next to each other was an enlightening experience. My first thought was, *Wow, these wonderful people who I had hoped would be our friends really are!* My second was, *This is just beautiful.* But my third thought was a little embarrassing for a guy who has studied the Bible for years, and who is such a big fan of Jesus: *Hey, I forgot about that verse!*

In the midst of all my worry about the many disasters that could befall, it had somehow slipped my mind that Almighty God might be deeply concerned about these same matters as I. If you had asked me, or told me, I would have given intellectual assent to this very foundational truth. Yet in my gut, it wasn't a question I was even asking.

Over the next few months I would look at that painting and try to focus my thoughts, try to release my grip, try to lay down my worry, try to believe that God was there to help. I guess these little pauses in front of the painting were short bursts of what the Bible and the mystics call "meditation." I kept praying and hoping and trying my best to trust that we would have a good outcome, while stopping short of demanding the same. I wanted to hold fast to the fact that God would "not forget" us, even as I tried not to define the terms of his care. When friends would say, "Everything will be all right," I would cringe and try to back away from what seemed like an overly hopeful and potentially soul-crushing expectation. After all, if God wanted to care for us on my terms, my son would have already been healed in utero.

Once the kids were born and we began our whirlwind life of daily hospital visits, I might occasionally pause to consider the painting and the thought behind it at the end of the day. Superstitious still, I wasn't quite ready to claim, or put too much hope in, some desired outcome. Yet I would judiciously recognize the slow progress we were seeing, and allow myself to imagine Will several years down the road, running around a playground with his sister. Yes, I would cautiously admit—and only to God—after the first few months of hospitalization, it did seem that things were getting better. The fog on the horizon was starting to clear.

When we all came home for good, the painting seemed to become richer, deeper, and clearer. Indeed, with us spending more time sitting around the living room, even the kids were starting to occasionally gape at it. We would be attempting to feed one of them, and their eyes would leave our face and fix on the painting, until their jaws would stop their rhythmic movement and we would have to gently remind them of the task at hand. If a little nudge didn't work, we might even shift our position so they couldn't see it so readily. Such interruptions should have frustrated us, but they usually made us smile and filled us with wonder. Somehow, it seemed our kids were entering into and living out of the reality to which the painting pointed: the kingdom realm that Jesus described where pedestrian concerns about food and clothing and housing melt away into a wholehearted, absolute trust in God's abundant minute-by-minute provision. Will and Ella were like the sparrows, and were calling us to join them.

On the night we returned home after Will's death, I stopped short of wanting to grab the painting and tear it up, but I did want to take it down or maybe cover it up with a black shroud to shade my eyes from its dissonant perspective. The words of the inscription suddenly seemed uncomfortable, painful even. I didn't want them to be true, because it seemed that if they were, I must have missed something. Had my faith been incomplete? Should I have prayed and meditated more frequently or more fervently? Had I, by my hesitations about claiming God's provisions, exempted myself from the grace so freely offered? Even in the midst of my grief, I realized that these were superstitions, plain and simple. If God had wanted, Will's life would have been saved, regardless of my faith, or practice, or naming-and-claiming of potential blessings.

The next day we were sitting around in our shock and utter emptiness. Outside, it was temperate and gorgeous, and we were enjoying the view through the open windows. And the most amazing thing happened: a tiny bird flew into one of the windows that had been swung open. It made exactly one lap of the room, passing by the painting before flying up into the skylight in the ceiling, where it repeatedly bumped its tiny head against the glass. In the same split second that I began to think about how I might help the bird find its way back out of our living room, it banked to the left, descended to window height, and promptly flew out the other window. The whole thing had taken less than thirty seconds, and we all blinked before verbally confirming it had really happened. In our surprise and laughter, my wife's mother—who had flown in to be with us—noticed a tiny white spot on the ottoman.

"I guess that God cares for even the sparrow!" someone exclaimed, celebrating the obvious reminder. We all turned to look at the painting. "Yeah," I offered more sarcastically, "God cares for us, but that doesn't mean we won't get pooped on!"

God's eye is on the sparrow. He values the sparrow, and treasures it, but he doesn't protect it, not always. Life brings poop, life brings pain, life brings death.

Later, I thought about how God's Holy Spirit is often depicted in the Bible as a bird that is always watching, ever present and caring for us all. Yet at the same time, for all of this help and care and love, the Spirit is not above leaving a little poo in the middle of our lives. Apparently our definition of *care* and *love* is often at odds with God's greater vision. The challenge, it seems to me, is to be expectant of his love without allowing ourselves to strictly define the terms of that love.

The image of the painting was featured on the funeral programs, and we displayed the work on easels at the front of the church. Not to put some bold stake in the ground, or to make an overarching statement of reality, or to make a grand claim that the darkness all around us was actually sweetness and light. It wasn't to deny anyone sadness, but to remind us that, even on that dark day, there was hope. Even when God seemed far away, God still cared. We put it up to remind us that we might someday have hope. We put it up to give ourselves something to reach for.

Black Tuesday

A few days after Will died, I realized that the actual story of his last few hours was at once unforgettable yet also subject to the shifting sands of memory. It was surprising to realize something so life-altering and iconic was nevertheless suffering from fuzzy details, missing elements, and subtle reinterpretations. Somehow, the questions I was asking about it in the rawness of my shock and grief were changing the story.

So I forced myself to sit down and write it out. To capture the experience and the attendant feelings, yes, but also to spare myself the burden of carrying it around inside my head. What follows is largely what I wrote, in the rawness of the shock and grief. I don't blame anyone for Will's death. On the contrary: I'm deeply indebted for all that everyone did for him, and am grateful that his presence at the hospital that night meant that he had every chance at life.

The call came from the cardiac catheterization lab on Monday at 9 a.m. The nurse said our heart-catheterization doctor and our kidney doctor had conferred about their competing concerns regarding Will's declining cardiac function and his emerging kidney troubles, and had agreed that they wanted to admit Will overnight for hydration. They would administer intravenous fluids, run some tests, and keep a close eye on him.

"How soon can you get here?" is a simple enough question, but it takes us a long time to feed and bathe everyone, load up and move out. By the time we got our kids and their clothes and supplies together, the big rush to get us admitted seemed to have passed and the updated request was for "sometime today, before 6 p.m."

Will had been enjoying his car rides less and less, and this trip had him screaming almost the entire way. For about thirty minutes he was sweating and crying and inconsolable. In the front seat, Stacy and I speculated that owing to the cardiologist's recent ultrasound evidence that Will's aortic arch was severely constricted, tomorrow's heart catheterization would probably end up being more cursory, and we hoped it would provide motivation to move the next heart surgery up a few weeks.

We arrived at the main admitting office at about 4 p.m., and they tried to figure out where we might go. The heart and kidney unit seemed the logical spot, but there didn't seem to be enough room for us. Stacy filled out a medical questionnaire, and when the admitting staff realized that Will had a persistent and contagious eye infection, they suggested he needed to be kept from the other patients. So the search for a private room only added to the wait.

We were told we'd get into the room as soon as they discharged the current patient and cleaned things up, but we weren't given any real time frame for this. It might be 30 minutes, or it might not be until 9 or 10 o'clock that night. In the meantime, there was really no quiet place to feed and comfort the kids, so both of them were pretty upset as we marked time in the waiting room and listened to the huge television blaring on about the 5th anniversary of the 9/11 terrorist attacks.

A little after 5 p.m. we were informed, "We're closing at 5:30. You'll have to find somewhere else." The staff was apologetic and promised a hospital-wide overhead page when the room became available. So we trundled the stroller, two fussing kids, two bulky car seats, and four bags down the hall. A few minutes later, Will was finally sleeping, Ella was still screaming, and Stacy needed a break and a chance to clean vomit off of herself.

By the time she returned from the restroom, my frustration had peaked. Why did we rush down here? Where were we supposed to go? With nothing else to do, I suggested we walk up to the catheterization lab to let them know we were there, and where to find us. Our nurse from the cath lab stomped and complained a little with us, made a couple of phone calls, and sent us up to our room: "Walk slow, 'cause they're just mopping the floor now! I'll be up later!"

The heart and kidney unit was a kind of homecoming as we talked with nurses who remembered us from our week there in June. They took us to a nice room at the very end of the unit, and we settled in. The admitting nurse made a kingly throne for Will, which he settled into with great comfort and quiet—and smiles all around. I was worried that he'd be unnerved by the new surroundings, but he was happy as could be.

The energetic nurse from the cath lab came up after her shift to welcome us and make sure we were doing well. Even better, she began the very important work of figuring out who were the "rockingest phlebotomists" on duty that night.

These are the coveted technicians who, by luck or expertise or sheer confidence, are known for their ability to introduce a needle to a vein. Will had always been a very tough "stick": between his small size and poor circulation, it was difficult to start an IV. So our nurse made some phone calls to arrange for a visit by "the best guy around" and promised to see us in the morning.

Our nurse in the HKU was only on duty until 11 p.m., but she set up the room and taught me how to use the feeding pump that was provided for us. We had previously experienced problems in getting timely feeds for our boy there, so we brought our own cooler for breast milk to feed him ourselves. Will took about twenty milliliters by bottle from his mother, which impressed us greatly, considering the day he was having.

We were happy enough to wait a couple of hours for the IV, since we didn't want a protracted and painful experience for Will. When the IV specialist came by, we were pleased, as he turned out to be one of our friends from the transport team. He arrived at about 9 p.m., placed a line on the second try, and drew blood for labs. Will screamed at full volume, of course, but settled down shortly afterward.

A bit later, the resident physician came by. She was a friendly, lovely and earnest doctor, but she seemed quite harried. Since neurology and cardiology share on-call time, she had two beepers that kept interrupting our conversation as she responded to inquiries via the phone in our room. Stacy gave her all the information about Will's conditions and meds and treatments. We were happy enough to work around the interruptions, but I was a little unnerved by her unfamiliarity with the specifics of our son's particular cardiac condition and the exact procedures for the hydration. As she left, I wished her a "quiet night," though I did inquire after the fact that we didn't have the IV fluids started yet. She promised to check on it.

Anxious as we were, the wait wasn't entirely negative. Will was in a remarkably charming mood. He had never smiled more, or had such a long period of interaction. He was talking and cooing. Looking from one person to the next, he shared that wide smile of his as his eyes twinkled. At one point he even leaned forward and let out a big belly laugh. His first laugh ever! We soaked it up.

But in time we realized it was getting late, and my wife and daughter needed to leave. Visiting hours were over, and it was frowned upon for us to keep Eleanor there overnight. So we staged a couple of photos of the babies in their coordinating outfits. Upon being laid next to her brother, Ella promptly jammed his hand in her mouth and started sucking away. As usual, Will didn't seem to mind. He was in his element up on that nest in his bed. Stacy held him for a few minutes to say good-bye, and when he started to fuss, she laid him on his side in the flat part of the crib to comfort him and ease any gastrointestinal discomfort he might have been feeling. His fussiness faded and he fell asleep. The two girls hurried out, mindful that they'd be hurrying back in just a few hours for the procedure in the morning.

I got Will's next meal together and quietly moved him, checking the placement of his feeding tube and starting his next meal. The nurses were changing shift, so I asked both the incoming and outgoing nurses about the IV fluids. A little later I saw the pump and the fluid bag, but it took another hour to find a pole on which to hang it.

At about midnight, when the fluids were finally hooked up, I started to relax and planned to give him one more feed before trying to get some rest myself. Problem was, Will was growing more restless, fussy, and increasingly hard to comfort. Normally, picking him up would provide at least a little calm, but this was different, and I puzzled at his discomfort. After a bit of troubleshooting, I decided his frustration was because of the IV in his foot and the accompanying board taped to his leg, so I tried my best to change his position in his bed, to talk to him and pat him as he lay there.

Soon, the monitor became the primary source of my frustration. We had been around cardiac/blood oxygen monitors for his whole life, but this setup seemed to be the worst we'd encountered. The parameters were set differently than we'd expected, and the alarms seemed especially loud. Our nurses were able to adjust some of the parameters according to the doctor's orders, but no one seemed to be able to change the volume. So the alarms were blaring away for respiration levels that weren't unusual to us, and the whole thing was obviously upsetting Will. Even more concerning was the ever-present problem of false alarms. His oxygen levels were reading at an alarmingly high level, but the numbers were so high (95–99 percent) that they seemed anomalous. Besides, these readings could sometimes be misleading when he was kicking and fussing, since the sensor can't get a good reading when it's jostled around. My frustration peaked again when his blood-oxygen saturation levels dropped to the mid-60s and a nurse came running from the central monitoring station to check on him.

"Is everything okay?" is perhaps not the best way to phrase a question to a bedraggled parent at 1:30 a.m. who's trying to comfort a now-hollering baby, and I'm sorry to say that this kindhearted person got a bit of a blast from me. Speaking over Will's loud voice, I suggested that things were not, in fact, okay.

"We ought to be concerned about these *high* blood-oxygen readings, but no one comes running when they're in the 90s. Now that he's back in his normal range in the 60s, you all act like there's a problem!"

To make a point, I again asked if there was anything that could be done about the volume, and then suggested that if these alarms were going to be bothering my son all night, we might just turn off the bedside monitor, since it was being watched at the desk anyway. She informed me the volumes were "locked in" and that turning the bedside monitor off would disable the central monitor. Which I'm sure was true enough. But it didn't help our conundrum: the more my son's monitor alarmed, the more he would cry, and the more he would cry, the more the monitor would alarm.

By now it was getting close to 2 a.m. and I was still awake and on my feet, very aware that Will would be getting un-fortified breast milk at the 3 a.m. scheduled feeding time, and so would be hungry shortly after that. I was also thinking about what a long day we had ahead of us and was anxious for both of us to get some sleep. My sense of frustration kept rising. I just wanted the monitor and the baby to be quiet so that we could rest. The nurse and I continued to confer about his restlessness and disconcerting monitor readings, and considered calling the doctor. But Will finally settled down a bit, so I lay down to catch a little sleep.

I woke up about 40 minutes later to the sound of his crying and saw that his nurse was trying to help him. His blood-oxygen levels were still ranging widely, and his breathing was more labored. We ran down the normal list of things: a new diaper, a new position, picking him up and putting him down, speculating he was just really overtired and simply needed to sleep. Still, she was concerned enough about him that she paged the doctor on call, who came quickly. We checked Will's oxygen again and tried to troubleshoot the problems we were seeing. Since it was right about 3 o'clock, I wondered if Will was hungry, so I grabbed a syringe to check his stomach contents via his nasogastric tube. The residual fluid in his stomach was mostly clear and of minimal volume, suggesting that his stomach was empty. I decided that a meal would settle him. Before I went to grab the milk, I leaned down to try to comfort him. He looked at me with a kind of middle-distance stare, seemingly content.

But when I stepped toward the cooler of milk, the nurse and doctor started to shout.

"This is real, isn't it?" the doctor said to no one in particular.

The alarms had been going off all night, sometimes because leads had fallen off or some such thing, but now the monitor was showing no breathing and no heartbeat. We later learned his breathing had stopped and that he had gone into complete asystole—no heart rhythm whatsoever.

They hit the "code blue" alarm and started CPR. Within what seemed to be seconds, the room flooded with people and I reflexively started moving furniture out of the way. A minute later, our nurse came alongside me to say that I might be asked to leave the room, so I stepped out into the hallway where there were even more people and a security guard who was shadowing me. A lot of people were asking me, "Are you okay?" It seemed like a silly question, even in my frantic state. I paced, watching the scene in the room through the window.

It was pretty chaotic in there. My wife later told me this is very common when a code team is responding. The doctor in charge of the team was at least a foot taller than everyone else, so I was able to see and hear him as he called for equipment and sent people to get an anesthesiologist, or a mask, or gloves, or whatever else was needed. When a piece of equipment was needed, a member of the team would go sprinting out of the room to return a minute later. So there was a kind of recovery area at the nurses' station, where people could sit on a trash can to catch their breath and where their coworkers could check on them and make sure they were all right. Even in my calmed panic, I noted the irony in front of me: so many hearts beating in the thin hope that one heart would somehow start again. It was surreal.

It seemed like time was moving very quickly and very slowly at the same time. I was desperately hoping for some sign of progress so that I could call Stacy. I didn't want to call her in the middle of a code; I wanted to tell her that Will had crashed but that he was back, or stabilized, or whatever.

Then the head of the team walked up to me in the hallway. He started forming some words, and I leaned in to hear, but they weren't registering. My legs were really weak, so I asked to sit down, and he helped me to a chair. A bunch of people craned their necks and cocked their ears while he talked to me. His breath was sour, like a man who had been working hard at running or lifting. He forced himself to slow down as he told me they weren't having much success, and that protocol was to move patients to the intensive care unit, where they would start ECMO (extracorporeal membrane oxygenation).

He wanted me to call my wife and confirm that this is what we wanted. I asked him to explain this more, and he said that ECMO was a complete heart/lung bypass meant to buy some time while a surgical team could be assembled. The intention of all this was to give Will's heart every chance to start again. I said "Okay," congratulated him on the successful intubation he had accomplished earlier with my son, and released him back into the room.

I called Stacy and woke her up. I told her that Will had coded and answered a few questions about how and when. I was trying to arrange a ride for her, since I didn't want her to drive. But she was insistent that she wanted to be there soon and she'd be all right. She didn't want to wait one minute longer than necessary. Before she hung up, she made me promise I'd call our friend Matt.

I reasoned that Matt interned as a hospital chaplain, that he lived close to the hospital, and that he'd have his phone on. But while it was ringing, the reality suddenly set in: I was waking up my best friend in the middle of the night from the hospital where my son was lying dead on the table and a code team was trying to bring him back. He answered with a sleepy "Hello." I croaked out some words, and he said he'd be right over.

Now the whole scene seemed more real, and I was up again and pacing. More people were asking if they could get me anything, and if I was okay. Which was bothersome to the point that I found myself engaging in imaginary conversations. *What would I want? And how could I be okay?* is what I screamed at them inside my head, but the noises that came out of my mouth sounded more like, "Thanks, I'm fine."

This was going on for a really long time. I kept looking in to see that someone was doing compressions, and I kept hearing the shouts for "another round of epi!" Finally the nurse came out to tell me they weren't having much success and that they might want me to come back into the room. Even in the middle of this, I noticed that everyone spoke tentatively—lots of "mights" and "maybes," and lots of references to some unidentified "them." The kind nurse put her hand on my shoulder to lead me in, but I wanted to walk in myself.

The crowd parted as I walked through the door, dumbfounded. I was expecting that he was dead, but a couple of people were still moving tubes around his face. I looked up to see the lead doctor. As he walked toward me, my ears tuned in for words of finality. But this was not to be a made-for-TV speech, because—and I'm forever grateful for this—he was *ticked off.* Freshly defeated and still livid, he was in shock himself. He rested his large hand on my shoulder, looked down at my face, and shook his head. "We tried everything . . . gave lots of meds . . . 15 rounds of epinephrine . . . but . . . I'm sorry . . ." His voice was failing. I leaned even closer and squinted my eyes so I could hear better. I was still waiting for the right euphemism. Finally it came: "He's passed away."

What?

The room cleared out then, except for two nurses I remembered from the cardiac ICU. The bed was pulled out at an angle in the middle of the room, so I walked around the head of the bed. I saw his face free of tubes, and then his hair. Oh, his hair, I thought, his beautiful hair! What a waste! I leaned in close, in utter shock. He was wrapped in a blanket that was spotted with blood, and his beautiful face was so still. The nurses asked if I wanted to pick him up, which I did. It seemed all at once to be very strange and ghoulish and yet perfectly appropriate.

Matt arrived soon afterwards and hugged both Will and me as deep sobs welled up from within me. Then I realized my phone was ringing—my wife. In shock I clicked off the phone so that I could gather myself. The nurses offered to clean up my son for his mother's arrival, and Matt and another really helpful lady helped me decide what to say to Stacy when I returned her call. In the end, I didn't tell her that Will was gone, and she didn't ask. I realized that, somehow, she already knew.

Back in the room, I picked Will up again and paced back and forth. This was unbelievable. What had happened? Had we missed something? Had I missed something? Had I done something wrong? How could all of this be over so quickly? It was overwhelming to think of all that he'd been through, only to have his life stop so short.

A few minutes later, our cardiologist came in. I was surprised to see her in the middle of the night. At the same time it only seemed appropriate to have her there. She was wearing scrubs, a hooded sweatshirt from her alma mater, and a pale expression of grief and shock. I'll always remember the way she walked toward me, saying nothing. Instead, she reached up to gather me and Will in one embrace. I sobbed hard into her shoulder for a minute before we separated and she gaped in disbelief and stroked Will's head.

Soon Stacy phoned me from outside the hospital, and Matt and I went down to the lobby to meet her. When she saw us, she said, "This is it, isn't it? This is it . . ." Matt and I both glanced at her and looked away, unable to maintain eye contact. We rode the elevator up to the 3rd floor and started walking down the hall. Matt took Ella in the stroller, and I ushered Stacy off to the side to tell her our son was gone. I followed her into the room and watched as she leaned over to look into his face. It was the absolute worst part of the whole experience: "Oh, my love . . . oh, my love," she wailed before she clutched him to her chest. The grief was too much to watch; I looked out the window in disbelief.

The next 5 hours were a blur. Our social worker got out of bed to come and sit with us, and she and Matt teamed up to help us in our initial shock and nascent decision-making. We held our boy and rocked him. We took a lock of his hair, a cast of his little hand, and inked two footprints. Doctors and nurses came by to express their condolences, their shock and their grief.

One of the most foreign ideas was that we were really done now. It took hours to sink into my brain: no cath, no second heart surgery, no lip closure, no 3rd heart surgery, no cleft closure, no nose repair, no more trips to the children's hospital. At the same time I felt a sense of relief for myself and for my son that we wouldn't have to go through all of that, which made me feel indescribably guilty. But mostly I couldn't imagine that we would really leave today. We'd walk out the door, without him, and be done.

What I desired most was an answer, to know what happened. Not that I needed someone to blame, and not that it would make any difference. And not that any of my desires mattered, anyway—I knew I wouldn't get the answer I was looking for. In a world of lawsuits and malpractice, I knew that I would never know. Which was just as well. It was a last gasp of control at an inherently uncontrollable situation and unexpected outcome, and it wouldn't change a thing.

Matt eased the transition by taking us to his home and giving us some space. He made us breakfast, lunch, and dinner, and let us toggle between wailing grief, laughter, phone calls, catnaps, and threadbare, comforting stories of our common friends and experiences. Our dear friend picked up my wife's mother from the airport, and they both sat with us all day, saying very little and listening lots and mostly just sitting through what must have been exceedingly uncomfortable silence.

At dusk, and against Matt's better judgment, we decided to return to a suddenly very empty home, where we stood in front of Will's lonely bed and wept and wept and wept.

Performance Art

As the days become weeks and the weeks become months following Will's death, I find myself wishing there were clearly understood cultural practices related to grief and mourning. I wish there were some social expectations of what people should do when they have suffered loss. This yearning is bigger than finding permission to wear black or to be sad all the time. This yearning feels as big as my whole life. Simply put, I wish I had something to do.

Standing in the shower today, it all hit me again. For just a second I seemed to float up above my life, and I remembered again that my son is dead. And in that moment of clarity I was inspired by a vision—an idea for expressing myself.

I wish I could find a house on a busy road somewhere. A moderate-sized, two-story structure. I'm thinking of a place with brick below and siding above, a lot of divided-light windows, and a good floor plan. With big trees scattered around the yard and an expanse of green grass leading up to a wide front door. Oh, and the driveway would lead around to the side of the house so that the garage door wouldn't be the typical eyesore it so often is. The place would look a lot like the ubiquitous house that every kid draws with crayons when they think of "home," complete with the smiling sun casting its rays from the upper left-hand corner of the scene.

And I'd be very patient and very neat and organized about it, and I'd get permission and permits and everything. Because what I'd like to do is to take that house apart.

Now understand, please: I'd be gentle. I wouldn't employ any violence—no fire or explosives or wrecking balls or bulldozers. I wouldn't be in any hurry and I wouldn't be angry. I promise I wouldn't even use a sledgehammer. I'm quite confident I could do the whole job with a single saw, my trusty Estwing framing hammer, and my battered blue crowbar. I'd just take that place apart, piece by piece.

Every single shingle, tile, casing, fixture, pipe, cabinet, and wire. Every door, every wall, every floorboard. Brick by brick, board by board, nail by nail. It would be a labor of love and devotion to take the house apart and methodically move it into neat piles in the front yard. Then, after many months of patient labor, I'd just leave that big, empty space there for everyone to see. They'd drive by on their way to work or the mall or whatnot, and say to themselves, "Hey, there was something valuable there before, and now there's not." People would feel something missing, and would feel a twinge in their gut and a question in their head. It would be like a piece of performance art.

Eventually, over time, I'd stop by to take a truckload of the pieces away. I imagine myself arriving in the morning, sipping on coffee from a thermos, and walking around to feel the space and breathe the air. Then I'd put on leather gloves and start throwing the pieces into the truck. I'd keep doing this every day, moving truckload after truckload of the stuff away, until the lot was completely empty.

Then I'd let the weeds and trees and greenery reclaim the space for a while. I'd let it be wild. A couple of years later I'd clean it up a little—mow the grass and clear out the brush—and make it into a park so that people could enjoy it.

It would be empty and full, all at once.

Brighter Skies

We live in northern Virginia, just a few miles from the Potomac River and Washington, DC, in a small apartment attached to a large house. I am a caretaker of sorts for the folks who live in the home, but our relationship would be best characterized as a friendship rather than employment. In our time here, they have cared for us, loved on our children, prayed for us, and put up with my general incompetence at gardening, which comprises the bulk of my responsibilities.

One of the highlights of this living situation is my newfound awareness of the land, plants, and weather, and the wonder of how sun and rain and snow and wind work together to nurture life. Of course, in the midst of our overwhelming responsibilities in caring for Will, and the disorienting grief that followed his death, my connection to the property became quite frayed. But as the waters of grief began to recede and I started to re-engage and catch up with my responsibilities, I took some time to contemplate the world around me. Since this new awareness dawned in the late fall and early winter, this awakening was a dark one. Everywhere I looked, I saw something that looked like death, but I knew that it wasn't— I knew that life existed beneath the brown grass, shriveled plants, and bare branches. I challenged myself to remember that although things looked bleak, life would return.

What follows are some thoughts that occurred to me at the time:

I love the fall—feeling the air turn crisp, and watching the shadows grow longer. It was a special treat this year to see the leaves turn their vivid hues and then fade and fall. I even enjoy the refreshing monotony of raking the leaves from their resting place to their spot at the curb, and I'm a little sad that the project is nearly completed.

Still, I'm forced to admit that on a gray day, things can look a little bleak. Without the foliage, the trees seem to reach up their fingers to pay homage to the broad, low, overcast skies. It looks like someone has shifted the whole landscape to sepia, and it feels like death. So we remind ourselves that it is *not* death but dormancy, that the life remains and thrives under the surface of things. We just need to wait for it to appear again, as it always does.

But on a clear day, like today, it is something to behold. The lack of canopy lets the bright and warming rays of sun flood through the windows, and the sharp sky tugs my heart upward.

A musician friend of mine, Ryan Sharp, penned "Brighter Skies, an Advent Song," in response to these thoughts. I found it brought further clarity to my reflections and was grateful for his gift to me.

Brighter Skies, an Advent Song

By Ryan Lee Sharp

I would follow you down
Pass through the sky to the ground

Floating, we'd not make a sound
I would follow you down

Well you left me this time last year
In the midst of our chaos and fear
Pieces by pieces disappear
Why'd you leave me this time last year?

With fingers pointed up to the sky
As if knowing I'm gonna ask why
But seasons have no alibi
With fingers pointed up to the sky

Silent you've seemed all this time
And if I knew it was the end, I'd be fine
But confusing is this death amidst this life
And silent you've seemed all this time

Maybe you'll appear once again
Pick me up and call me friend
It's a rhythm I can't comprehend
Still I'm hoping you'll appear once again

Still I'm hoping you'll appear once again
Oh come back to me, come back to me, friend
Oh come back to me, come back to me, friend

This song said more to describe my sense of loss and disappointment, of confusion and chaos, and of alienation and abandonment by God than anything I could say. Where I tend to hint at such frightening things obliquely, Ryan walks right over and embraces the full, fearful truths. Where I would feel God's silence or God's distance, but not dare to admit it, my friend just opens all of that messiness up for me to see and sing and own.

I was sharing this one night with a group of folks from church, who gather to get to know each other better and help one another down the path to wholeness. I was talking about how in the past I used to offhandedly throw out the line, "If you're feeling far from God, it's not because God has moved!" to suggest that God is unmovable and constant and completely available to us, while we sinful creatures are prone to wander. But I was reconsidering that statement just then. To the best of my recollection I hadn't gone anywhere, but it seemed God had. I hadn't stopped asking God questions, but God didn't seem to be answering them. And as I was talking about this, about my intention to find a way to wait, hoping God would "come back to me," I realized I might be a little misguided, that I might be rushing things. Maybe it is kindness and love and mercy and grace that are behind God's frequent silence and apparent distance. Maybe God knows that any sense of closeness and connection would be too painful just now, stuck as I am in the cold of winter with questions that don't have answers, or at least that don't have any comforting answers. Maybe this cold and quiet season is something natural, necessary, and to be weathered in due time.

Breath of Life

I know it is exceedingly common for new parents to worry that their sleeping children have stopped breathing. So many worries about sudden infant death syndrome (SIDS) have been added to the instinctual worries of generations of parents, and enough Back to Sleep public-relations campaigns have been circulated that it is hard for people to resist obsessively checking their sleeping babies, to the point that we risk waking them up every fifteen minutes. Plus, it is so indulgently satisfying to see that they are, in fact, alive, and to revel in their placid calm. Makes you feel like the world might not be such a bad place, after all.

And of course we're no different. My wife and I are always straining our ears to hear if our daughter is climbing out of her crib, or if she might be choking or smothered or something. We'll stare at her in the faded light to see her chest rise or to detect some other movement. "Can you check on the girl and see if she's breathing?" one of us will ask the other. "She's breathing, and she's alive," is our coded comment that erases the worry from the other's face, at least for a little while.

Since the kids were born, we've shared this concern-bordering-on-obsession with our friends, who always say, "I know what you mean!" But I'm afraid they don't. Within several hours of Will's birth, we backed away from his bed in the neonatal intensive care unit, in the hospital where he was born, while alarms blared and a team of doctors, nurses, and respiratory specialists tried to get him breathing again. His heart was beating erratically, but his lungs were still. Everyone was rushing around in the forced calm that comes over medical professionals when they know they shouldn't be panicking themselves, and shouldn't worry the parents. After what seemed like ten minutes but which must have been much less, they finally relaxed a little and stopped squeezing the supplemental oxygen bag, and he was breathing on his own again. After a few more of these episodes of apnea, we agreed to have him intubated (where a tube is put down his throat to his lungs) and placed on a mechanical ventilator. This was the first of many choices that rushed at us, which didn't seem as difficult in the moment as I had expected.

After his heart surgery, he was even more dependent on a mechanical ventilator, a machine that basically breathes for the patient. It mixes a prescribed percentage of oxygen with purified air, delivering it in precise rhythm through a tube. Since the air goes directly to the lungs (bypassing the mucous membranes of the mouth and airway), it is important that it be humidified, so sterile water is vaporized into a mist that combines with the carefully mixed air traveling through a large ribbed tube and into a smaller endotracheal tube that goes down the throat.

Anyone who has ever watched a foggy window on a cold morning can guess what inevitably happens. With unnerving regularity we would watch helplessly as the vaporized water in the humidified air would condense, and a few drops would slide down the ET tube. That's when I learned the term *vasovagal response*, which describes the state of depressed heart rate and breathing that reflexively engages when a person inhales liquid. Which results in a simple cough and recovery, if you are upright and able-bodied. But if you're flat on your back and breathing through a tube, recovery is not so simple. In those excruciating moments, the nurse would call for assistance and hurry to disconnect the ventilator and suction the tube with another smaller tube. Then supplemental oxygen would be attached to the tube, and someone would squeeze the attached bag to try to engage his breathing again. There were many occasions when we stood helplessly by the bedside, waiting for the outcome: death, or life. It is a troubling experience. There is absolutely nothing to do but wait and watch. To worry and hope. To wonder what you will do if he doesn't bounce back.

And then there was the night when we never took that deep breath of relief. They worked and worked, and all the drugs and dedication and expertise and effort in the room couldn't change the outcome. We sat by his body for hours and waited for his chest to rise or his eyes to move, until the reality finally sunk in that he was really gone.

So even now I worry over Ella not breathing. Moreover, because I've lived through the worst outcome, I expect in some way that she won't be breathing—I prepare myself that way. Sitting at the kitchen table, typing just now while I listen in vain for any movement or sounds from her crib, my mind embraces this unequally yoked construction: she might be dead, for real—that could have already happened. At the same time, I'm aware that if I go back there right now to check, I'll probably wake her up. In my head, the possibilities of her being either asleep or dead are equal, and I accept this possibility in the same manner that I accept the fact that a semitruck might run us over on the highway this afternoon. Or it might not. Probably won't, in fact.

So, is she sleeping or is she dead? If I go back, I'll wake her up. But by the time I go back there, if she hasn't been breathing, then she really will be dead. I never resolve this conundrum; I just try to keep breathing and waiting. Every time her eyes open, I feel an overwhelming sense of relief and joy. In a very dark way, losing her brother has made me even more grateful for the simple gift of life.

The other day, the three of us who are left were heading to some destination. Ella and I descended the stairs out of our apartment. We rounded the corner to the car, got situated and strapped in, adjusted the mirrors, and played some music. "Where is Mommy?" I asked my girl, half expecting an answer. The whole escalation of fear I was experiencing probably took seconds rather than minutes, but my worry was increasing at an exponential rate. Finally I was concerned enough to leave Ella to check on her mother. By the time I ran around the corner, cell phone in hand, I had already decided and accepted that my wife had suffered a heart attack, and fully expected to see her laid out on the walk. The only question in my mind was, What would I do? What was the American Heart Association's latest procedure for CPR? How long would it take the paramedics to arrive? Would I be allowed to take Ella in the ambulance (without a car seat), or would I need to follow behind in our car? Would I be able to drive, or would one of the paramedics drive my car for me?

I saw my wife descending the stairs, and I think we were both shocked at my tearful reunion with her. "I thought you were dead!" I said in wonderment. I hugged her, leaning over to press my cheek against the back of her head. "I'm so glad you're okay!" When I finally pulled back, she just smiled and gazed with moist eyes, reminding me that I'm not alone in my desperation and fear, or my newfound awareness of the fragility of life.

Give and Take

When you're feeling lost, it's nice to gather with folks who have a better sense of direction and a more settled view of the landscape. This is one of the main reasons, I think, that community is so valuable. When we can't pray, those who are journeying with us can pray for us. When we don't know what to do, others can help us. When we're bereft of even emotion, our friends can cry for us. When we don't feel like being thankful or gracious, our neighbors can speak on our behalf. And when we're so impossibly self-absorbed that we can only think of ourselves, we can pray for and serve others.

This I affirm, and much more. Yet standing among the assembled faithful one Sunday morning, I found myself singing "Blessed Be Your Name" (by Matt Redman), feeling utterly alone.

I managed to make it through most of the song on autopilot, appreciating the instrumentation and following the PowerPoint slides as they clicked past on the screen. But when we got to the phrase "You give and take away," with all of its repetitions, I woke up to what I was singing.

Here I was, gathered with friends, blithely noting the capricious hand of God. I was pledging to accept all that God gives, and everything that God takes away, in the same manner.

To stand with Job in the desolate wasteland of a suddenly empty life and share his counterintuitive and crazy construction, "Though he slay me, yet will I trust in him" (KJV). I was blessing God, in spite of this painful and unwelcome treatment of me.

When I heard myself, I stopped singing and looked around. I was standing in a roomful of zombies, or so it seemed. How else could I explain a bunch of people cheerfully singing praises to a God who alternately blesses us and stands by while we suffer? Who were these people? Why were they still singing, and smiling? Hadn't they felt any crippling pain? Hadn't they ever lost anything or anyone? Or had they just forgotten about it? Or, worse yet, were they so disassociated that their singing was unrelated to their lives?

We might do better to sing "Pain feels good!" to some chipper tune, again and again. That'd be more honest. Or maybe just call what is painful, good, and what is good, painful. Maybe we should all just pray, "Hey, whatever you want to do, God! It's all fine with me!" Or to rename God as Fate, and just smilingly accept whatever comes our way. While we're at it, shouldn't we give lobotomies in the church lobby? I mean, what kind of person would offer the same response of "Bless you!" to a gift of a gold watch, or a sledgehammer to the teeth? Such a person would be a psychological anomaly on the order of a sociopath. What is more strange: for me to fantasize about singing "Leave me alone, God," or to mindlessly mouth words of blessings in the face of suffering?

Are we supposed to be so stalwart, so heavenly minded, so focused on the ever-after, that we treat our lives as merely illusory? To keep repeating the apostle Paul's old saw, "Consider it pure joy, my brothers and sisters, whenever you face trials of many kinds," until we've propagandized ourselves to the point we don't feel any pain? Are we coming up short of God's hopes for us if we simply tell God that we don't appreciate the turn our life has taken? Though he slay me, yet will I offer a polite rejoinder?

Still, I didn't walk out, or grab the microphone, or stand in silent protest. I cleared my throat, took a breath, and rejoined my sisters and brothers in song. Because their words are true. Indescribably painful, but true.

Medical Missionaries

Have you ever had the experience of seeing someone where they aren't? I find it happening frequently at airports, and especially when I've moved to a new town. I'll be going about my day and I'll catch a glimpse of the back of someone's head, or their profile, or maybe I'll just see someone in my periphery. And my brain matches that person with a similar person in my mental photo directory. So I'll be in Houston and see one of my friends from Minnesota. Or I'll be unloading the moving van in a new town and recognize one of my old neighbors. Except that, when I blink and look again, it's not that person at all. My brain fills in the blank spot as it tries to find a familiar place in the world.

After two intensive months of daily visits to the hospital, those doctors, nurses, techs, managers and maintenance staff seem so familiar that they impose themselves in other places. Even though it's been more than six months since our discharge, those faces are so burned into my consciousness that I recognize them all the time. Most days that I come to this coffeehouse to write, I catch myself staring at a barista who is tall and dark, of scruffy beard and broad shoulders and with a slight slouch, just like the leader of the code team that tried to bring Will back. Probably once a day I see someone who I think is our cardiologist. In a second, I'm happy to see this person who seems like a close friend. In the next second, I think about ducking around a corner because I couldn't possibly talk to her. And in the next second I realize it's not her, after all. And thinking about it just now, I suddenly realize she's not our cardiologist, not anymore.

All of which might explain my recent experience in front of the television. As is our usual custom, my wife was running the remote, and I was along for the ride. She happened upon one of those touching educational/experiential stories about children facing medical problems in the early days of their lives. The particular patient featured on the program was actually two: conjoined twin baby girls. Connected at the front of their chests and abdomens, we quickly learned via 3-D computer image that they each possessed their own vital organs, though their livers were overlapping to the point of interconnectedness, and their hearts, while distinct, were inexplicably beating with the exact same rhythm. So their separation surgery would be fascinating, intense, and multidisciplinary.

But the thing that got my wife to set down the remote was the venue. It was "our hospital." Indeed, as the camera followed the family through the halls, and panned the large conference room, and visited the intensive care unit, we saw face after familiar face. And there was none of the expected searching for names, either—seeing even the corner of a face brought about an almost involuntary recitation of their names as we listed off the folks who had helped us so much.

Seeing them on the screen, I felt honored to know such amazing people, doing such miraculous work for families with nowhere else to go. They stand at the very top of their fields and yet perform their work with compassion and humility. I smiled as I watched, happy to know them and pleased that I could recognize them.

And then, quite unexpectedly, I found myself crying. I didn't know why, but tears were rolling down my cheeks as my head swiveled back and forth on its own, a silent *no* of some deeper protest. My wife noticed this and offered to change the channel, but I waved her off. I couldn't look away, not now. I had to watch. I tried to search my consciousness for some reason that this was so compelling. It wasn't that I was worried about the survival of the twins—I knew the producers wouldn't put this on TV if there was a bad outcome of the surgery. It wasn't that I was concerned for the parents—I actually felt rather callous as the father applied cold logic to the situation and the mother came emotionally unhinged just before the surgery.

The experience of saying good-bye to your child, perhaps for the last time, felt familiar to me, and I didn't find much empathy or pity in my feelings. Instead, I just viewed the parents sending their children to the surgical suite as a shared experience, much like the way I'd relate to a person who also had their car stolen, or who'd suffered from shin splints after too much running—as someone who had gone through something painful but not uncommon. I watched the surgery with interest and saw the expected reunion and recovery in the ICU, but I didn't feel especially connected to the parents or the kids.

What I did feel were tears dripping off my chin every time one of the cardiologists was on-camera, or the chief of radiology, or the amazing plastic surgeon, or anyone else I recognized. In my mind, those people still *belonged to us*. Granted, I always knew they had other patients, and families and friends and lives. I mean, I never expected that they would sit with us in the cafeteria, or take a personal interest in our lives, or would stop to talk to us in the hallway (though this happened frequently). At the same time, that was *Will's* sonographer, *Will's* respiratory therapist, *Will's* fan from housekeeping, *Will's* nurses, *Will's* hospital administrator. They belonged to us, and we to them. Except for one thing:

Will was gone. This connection, this critical link, was missing. The gap between us was deep and dark. I wished that I had him back, of course. But failing that, I wished I had the strength to go back and thank them for their ministry to us.

I was glad that these heroes were working their stations before we needed them, and that they'll continue long after we stop imagining we see them when we get coffee or groceries. I was glad they aren't defeated by death, and that they take on each new patient with professionalism and hope. I was thankful such brilliant and dedicated people devote themselves to something so good and loving as caring for helpless children and their even more helpless families.

Maybe I was a little jealous: envious that they were not still working on our Will. Or maybe I wished someone would make a television show about my boy. To remember a story that didn't turn out quite so well, and to pay tribute to these medical missionaries who loved him, truly. To show the anger they felt, and the tears they shed, when he died. And to show, in some way I cannot imagine, how they turned from that deathbed and went on to help their next patient.

My Psalm

I once had a business acquaintance ask me an unexpected question: "Where are you from, anyway?" It was a friendly inquiry, to be sure. So I shared that I'm from the Midwest—Illinois and Iowa. Had she detected my accent?

"No, it was the fact that you're so polite," explained this native New Yorker, typically direct. "You're always saying 'I'm sorry' and 'please' and 'would you mind?' and 'thank you.'"

It's true. Deference, good manners, putting others before myself, and being self-deprecating to build others up—these are all deeply ingrained parts of who I am.

So I'm a little worried. I know it is acceptable to be angry with God. I know it's good to be honest with God. I tell people that very thing all the time. It's part of having a real relationship. Would you want your spouse to only kowtow to your wishes? Would you want your best friend to avoid ever telling you the truth? Would you want your child to blindly accept everything you do and say?

So when I'm upset about something, I try to be honest with my Creator. I'll even use profanity if I feel like it (not *at God*, but about the situation). But I'm afraid I'm still avoiding a painful confrontation. That I'll never do it or that I'll crowd in so many qualifiers, justifications, theological caveats, introspective comments about my own selfishness, and alternate perspectives that I'll never get out the big, fat, ugly truth. That I'll coyly quote lyrics and poems of others who have had the courage to look up at God and say what they think. That I'll list Bible verses and exegete imprecatory Psalms, but never speak for myself. That I'll avoid ownership of my true feelings by hiding them in my own attempts at poetry.

Following is my best attempt at an honest and earnest Psalm to God:

God, what good are you? What earthly good?

Why do some of us have to grovel for stuff that other people receive completely apart from any effort or expense?

Some people beg for babies, while others can't be bothered to give birth to their kids. Some people work for and pay for and suffer for healthy bodies, while others squander their perfect health.

And then, why are the objects of our affections so routinely taken from us? Poets ponder the relative advantages of loving and losing, but everyone knows they both hurt like fire. Why is this?

So what are you up to?

You might be powerful, but what good does that do? When is your power exercised? You might be good, but toward what end?

Whether high above or flowing through the fabric of our lives, what good does your goodness do?

You might know the past and future, but to what benefit? How does that help anyone, when you're so quiet?

Loving my son was one of the most selfless things I've ever experienced.

That love was a gift from you—of this I'm quite sure. So, what's the point?

Why give me that love, and that boy, and that life, and then take it away? Why let me go through all of the wrenching heartbreak?

Moreover, why let him go through all the pain and misery? Why should he suffer, and why should I be forced to watch?

Why should I learn all about caring for him, and commit to that—to really put my shoulder to something important, for once—only to have it crumble?

Why leave his twin sister alone, and his mother in abject misery, clutching his empty body, rocking back and forth, saying, "My love, oh, my love . . . oh, my love . . ."

If you can look at that, I'd have to call you heartless, because—cold as I can be—I couldn't look at that. I couldn't watch that.

That's just some kind of cruel nightmare.

You give us these hearts, and then you break them.

And we spend a lifetime trying to explain away this simple fact: you could do something, and you don't.

So what good are you?

Anger

I have a friend who lives just a few minutes from our place, and she is the gracious host to many church meetings at her home. These always happen in the evenings, and so my route to her house is affected by rush-hour traffic. I take a larger, well-traveled thoroughfare to her house, avoiding the more direct yet stoplight-riddled route and its jam of commuter traffic. But late at night, when the meetings are over, I'm free to go straight home.

And therein lies the issue: the direct route goes right by the funeral home. So when I make the fateful left turn down that road, it is with the awareness that I'm about to cause myself some pain. Just to emphasize the effect, I usually dial up U2's "Pop" on the iPod and skip forward two songs. This postmodern, postindustrial marvel of an album with its mix of faith and doubt, of hope and pain, of irony and honesty, of heaven and earth has provided much support over the past year. Even now I find the techno sounds to be the perfect melancholy background as I contemplate the life that was both enabled and ended by technology.

This third song, with its driving techno beat, synthesized sounds, and slightly distorted lyrics speaks of a man trying desperately to find his way in the world. He's searching for salvation, for the means to fill that God-shaped hole within, and later, for the baby Jesus "under the trash."

Then the drumbeats and driving bass lines subside, and a clear, plaintive voice rises above a synthesized bed of sound. The singer wails to his mother, who died when he was a child.

I'm driving by the funeral home now, looking at the perfect brick structure, its steeply gabled roof, and its neat parking lot. It is so still, so quiet, so empty. I think: The employees must drive the vans and vehicles home at night, because there's never more than one vehicle parked out front. But the hearse must be in back; no one would drive that, would they?

I think of the basement, where his body spent the days before and after the funeral. I think of the other basement, the one at the hospital. No one thinks about a morgue at a children's hospital, not until it's too late. I went everywhere with my son, but I never went into these subterranean spaces where death presides.

The song picks up again and crowds the sonic space with more layers of instrumentation and background vocals, until I lean forward to listen to the lyrics buried in the crescendo— words the singer directs to his mother, father, brother, and sister: "*soothe* me, *rule* me, *fool* me, *woo* me . . ."

I cringe at this summary of our family. My nurturing wife, my embarrassing tendency toward structure, Ella's charming smile, and Will's many struggles. When the medical teams were doubtful, he would soldier on. When they were hopeful, he would stumble into an unforeseen setback. He overcame almost everything, until finally he quite suddenly stopped, and each of those same medical professionals came to his bedside, hollow eyes betraying utter shock, shaking their heads and saying over and over again, "I can't believe it."

I'll generally skip forward then to the last song on the album, "Wake Up Dead Man," a kind of rock ballad with spare, conventional instrumentation and a single voice. Except this understated song contains some withering lyrics as the singer laments the broken world presided over by a Savior who is too often silent.

Honestly and sincerely outlining the dilemma we all face: If God is real, and good, and powerful, then why doesn't God do more to help us? Despair and hope are weaved together until the singer wonders if perhaps there's order in all the disorder.

I've long noted the anger I feel in the ten-minute drive home, the tears I cry, and the way I need to compose myself before tiptoeing into the house. But last night I felt the weight of the "fool me, brother" more than usual and realized I'm angry at my son and the way he tricked us.

He was the smallest success story of one of the world's greatest pediatric cardiac teams, a three-pound wonder who miraculously survived and recovered from an extended battery of surgical and medical interventions. When during the first surgery they needed to induce hypothermia and completely stop his heart and circulation, the time stretched out to fifty-nine minutes—just under the surgical team's absolute maximum allowance of sixty minutes. Everyone waited to see what such an extended lack of oxygen would mean for his other organs and his brain, and he slowly and steadily relieved us of those concerns. Though surely possessing cognitive and physical deficits, he was, on the whole, just fine. He tripled his weight as he grew into an interactive, bright, and expressive little boy. And yet, upon his return for a relatively simple exploratory heart-catheterization procedure, he just stopped breathing. And I was angry at him for doing so.

I was angry for his leaving us, and for letting me stand there and watch it. I was angry for his doing it when his mother was not around to say good-bye. I was angry for his leaving his sister and not hanging around to meet all of his great-grandparents and cousins and other family. I was angry that his departure means I'll always be incomplete. I'll always hesitate when asked, "How many children do you have?" I'll always be unsure about how to talk about him to his sister, always worried I'll make too much or too little of his short life.

How messed up is that? I mean, he ought to be angry with *me*, for the way in which my choices caused him pain. In fact, I stew in this self-flagellation regularly, recounting what my desperate decisions meant for him; what they cost and what pain they brought. But this time I admitted a new feeling: anger, directed at Will. "How could you leave us, Will?" I whispered into the air. "What are we supposed to do now?"

This is so cliché, so Kübler-Ross, I thought. Blaming my son for his departure. I must be going crazy. But the feeling remains, in spite of my chastisement of myself: I'm angry with my son, and I don't know what to do about it.

I'm sorry, buddy.

Middle-Distance Stare

Triage

A French term *triage* is usually applied to hospital or battle-field situations, where the injured are sorted according to medical priority. Those injured the worst are assigned first, those injured least are assigned last, and those too grievously injured are not assigned at all.

I suppose I'm not unusual in that much of my education came through television. Before I ever looked up a formal dictionary definition, my introduction to the concept of triage came through the long-running series $M^*A^*S^*H$, where army physicians would care for the wounded at a mobile hospital located quite close to the battlefield. In a scene repeated almost endlessly, the surgeons were rousted from sleep or boredom or revelry to run outside into the camp's common area to perform triage before heading into the surgical tent to begin the surgical procedures. Typically the doctors would be kneeling in the dirt, peeking under bandages, arguing with one another about whether a particular patient should be put first in line or not in line at all. And the climactic line of dialogue would go something like this: "Sure, I *might* be able to save him, if I commit two surgeons to a five-hour operation.

But in the meantime, those three patients will *definitely* die." Impossible choices made in impossible situations.

Something similar happens in every emergency room as patients with allergies and colds and cuts and bruises are left in the waiting room for hours, while those with gunshot wounds and heart attacks are attended to first. In such cases, it is good to be passed by—it means you're in the best shape and need the least care.

The same scenario played out for us in the cardiac intensive care unit, when the families of new patients would follow the transport team down the hallway and through the doors to the unit itself. In their tunnel-vision haste they would unknowingly rush by the battle-weary families in the waiting room, and would invariably press the staff to understand why their child wasn't getting their operation *today*, only to hear again and again that the operations happen when necessary, but that they must always happen for the worst cases first.

If your child can wait, you must take it as a sign of their (relatively) good health. Of course, all of us—no matter how seasoned—felt slighted if our kid was bumped down on the surgical schedule, or if a shortage of beds required that she be moved from the elite cardiac ICU to the more general care of the pediatric ICU. But in time we all recognized that such a move was actually a compliment to our child. He or she was strong enough to wait or to do with lesser care.

And eventually each of us who made that understandably self-absorbed walk down the hall, by the waiting room, and past the other eleven beds to the one set aside for *our child* would come to the embarrassing realization that the inconsiderate people who are sleeping in the waiting room and leaving their food sitting around and watching the TV with the volume entirely too high are in fact *families*, suffering much the same as every other family, coping in the best way they know how. They too were doing triage, choosing presence over appearance, eating bad food, smelling rather funky, and sacrificing family and employment and dignity to care for a beloved child.

In less urgent and dramatic ways, triage happens in our everyday lives, when we focus on an emergency at the office, or work right through lunch, or forgo sleep to sit with a sick child, or when we borrow money to pay the bills. In a crisis, everything rushes by in a blur, and you make the most important decisions, as you must. We make the difficult, costly choice now, and know we'll need to pay for it later.

Depending on the level and length of the crisis, that payment might come in the form of post-traumatic stress disorder. This is a term from psychology that describes the time that comes after the crisis, when your brain has the luxury of slowing down and reliving the stuff you didn't have time to think about earlier, to experience the feelings you were too shocked to feel. The information and feelings that were too painful or too impossible before now get played over and again on the big screen, high-definition TV in your mind—the one that can rewind and slow-mo and even stop-action our most painful, most shameful, most difficult moments.

For a time I'd lie in bed most every night, unable to sleep. My eyes would dart around behind their lids as I revisited and reenacted that same chronology, that same Black Tuesday. Almost as if in a dream, tiny details would crop up like a splinter in my brain. They were pieces of the narrative that would need to be placed in context before I could find some peace.

> What was the last thing I said to him?
> Why did I put his milk back in the cooler?
> How did I have the phone number to call my friend?
> What did the doctors say?
> What did I say?

Why did I move the furniture out of the way?
Where did I put it?
How did I let this happen?

Once I had sufficiently reconstructed that night, my lightened brain was free to explore other parts of the previous year. Each revisiting seemed to expand the breadth of the memories as my mind rewound the film just a little further each time so that as the calendar moved forward, the memories went further back.

Owing mainly to his cleft lip and palate and severely compromised cardiovascular function, feeding was always an issue with Will. During the days, at least, we would offer him a bottle after which we would give him the balance of his meal via a feeding tube. So we were constantly seeking a fine balance between *pushing him to do just a little more* and *letting him rest* and get his calories by tube. Looking back, it's easy to wish we had been easier on him, but we were trying to make the best choices out of long-term concerns for his health and development.

On several vivid occasions we held him down while we pushed that same feeding tube up his nose, down his throat and into his stomach, with him coughing and sputtering and screaming all the way. We were trained to let him scream for a few seconds, then advance the tube when he would stop to swallow, which just seems cruel in retrospect. Once it was properly placed, we would then tape it—along with his oxygen tube—to his face so he wouldn't pull them off. When he did get ahold of them and pulled them down around his mouth, we'd often not notice until his blood-oxygen level fell below the alarm limit. At which point we'd do our best to gently push and pull everything back into its proper location, that very same spot where it always sat, which was why he wanted to pull the tubes away in the first place.

The recollecting goes on and on. A hundred routines, played out over thousands of repetitions as we cared for him at home. Routines like forcefully burping him, elevating his head in his bed, clearing his airway of vomit, providing oxygen (and so learning to distrust the regulator on the tank), and the swabbing and cleaning of his eyes as we treated his persistent eye infections.

All completely normal, and yet all seem harsh in the clearer light of memory. Looking at photos and videos now, I see the many ways in which we gently restrained his arms. Since he was relatively uncoordinated and small, simple barriers of blankets and soft toys were an effective way of keeping him from grabbing at tubes, but I knew that a day would come when his coordination would be more developed, and where he'd be postoperative and in danger of pulling IVs or sutures and so would require restraints on his arms and legs. I accepted this with barely a blink and would occasionally glance over at other children strapped to their beds, though I'm horrified at such acquiescence now.

And what about the hospitals? My tolerance of a three-pound baby in constant pain (who stands by while their child is given morphine?), blithely looking through his open sternum at his heart, snapping photos, celebrating as the sutures healed so quickly, and watching again and again as IVs were placed in his arms, legs, groin, and even his scalp. It is easy to forget about the torturous decision to have the surgery in the first place—of signing the line that meant pain and difficulty for a beloved and innocent child.

And what of leaving? Other parents would sit by their child's bed all day, every day, leaving only to eat in the cafeteria and sleep in the waiting room. I told myself that we couldn't, that we needed to take care of our other child. But now I wonder if, given other circumstances, I would have been dedicated enough to stay so close to him, or if I was distancing myself from his pain. How could I leave him like that? I could never leave my daughter overnight with someone, even now.

The rewinding goes back even further as I remember that the hospital was also the primary venue for our investigation, and possible intervention, of the pregnancy itself. So many ultrasounds that their memories all run together, consultation with genetics doctors, early connections with our social worker, and learning that the cafeteria's corn bread was not only cheap but tasty. These explorations were mostly speculative, as any interventions or even chromosomal testing would have constituted an unacceptable threat to the other baby in utero. In the end, all of this study and consultation was helpful for our own preparation, though it raised far more questions than it answered.

Some days I even think all the way back to our many fertility interventions. Of simple testing, which led to minimally invasive intrauterine insemination. Which, with its ineffectiveness, led to the more invasive and much more expensive in vitro fertilization—the harvesting and subsequent fertilization of ovum in a laboratory, a decision not made lightly or with complete certainty.

Should we have just taken the great cosmic hint from God and adopted, or remained childless? Is all of this our fault somehow? Here, my brain skips across the chronology to scoop up the fact that post-birth genetics testing proved that his abnormalities were developmental rather than chromosomal. So what was happening on the days or weeks around these formations? What about that fateful decision to implant two embryos instead of one? Was it selfish or selfless for us to want to have children of our own?

In the moment, we do what we must. But just as in the fable of the tortoise and the hare, our questions and doubts slowly, inexorably catch up to our quick decisions.

Projection

Anyone who has been through any significant difficulty will hope that they have family, friends, *community*. These are the people who feed you meals, wash your clothes, carry your burdens, and wipe your tears. They are indispensable and irreplaceable. We cannot imagine slogging through our misery without them.

At the same time, anyone who has community gathered around them will cringe at an unavoidable byproduct: *projection*. In the case of my wife's and my journey, our dear friends walked with us through heartbreaking infertility, exciting pregnancy, threatened miscarriage, bed rest, birth, brand-new twin babies, breast-feeding, and the extended, serious illness of a loved one. And eventually they saw us through death, loss, and grief. Those who have been through similar experiences will understand the twin feelings of love and anger, of connection and alienation, of intimacy and isolation that go with such community. Like a gathering of family for a holiday dinner, there is a tangible affection combined with an infrequent, almost unbearable irritation at those who are so beloved.

People mean well, of course. But we're all still human and so we're fallible and susceptible to the unintended barbs of others. The worst of which is projection. You know you're about to suffer the dreaded projection when you hear this statement torpedoing through the stormy waters of your life toward you, and brace yourself for the impact: "Oh, I know what you mean."

Now, gentle reader, if you've ever been in that position, you know your only option at that point is to nod and smile. Wipe your tears and gather yourself together. It may be that your friend has just tried to switch places with you—that they are hoping to switch from *helper* to *helped*—or it may be the case they're sincerely trying to connect with you in the best way they know. But know this: In that moment, you cannot say what you most desperately long to say.

So let me say it for you. Maybe then we'll both feel better. When someone says, "Oh, I know what you mean!" and proceeds to offer some antidote or some anecdote from their own life (or something they read in *Reader's Digest*, or some book their aunt Midge once told them about), you want to tell the truth—you want to say, "No, you don't," or perhaps a more gentle, "Actually, my situation seems a bit different from that." Or at the very least, you'd like to offer a feeble, "Well, not exactly." But you can't. You're stuck now with the embarrassment of your situation, and the misery of your own confusion and pain, and the nagging thought that you might be anywhere other than right here, right now, hearing about someone else's misery when you can scarcely believe your own.

Projection is, at its root, relating everything to yourself: your experience, your life, your pain, your kids, your pregnancy, your child rearing, your loss, your grief, and your means of coping. And while all the stuff you've been through is important and valuable, and gives you empathy and reference points for my pain, it is still yours. And mine is mine. So please, be thinking of and reflecting on what you've known and experienced and learned. Please remember the feelings you've experienced and let them be a bridge of empathy to connect us. But please, think twice—no, thrice—about saying it out loud.

Yes, I know it's hypocritical for me to mention it here, and unkind for me to suggest I don't want to hear about your life. Moreover, I know you have very likely been through something much worse than I and in fact have a lot to teach me. But please, if you're sitting with me in my raw pain and swirling confusion, and if you'd like to help me, then let's talk about *me*. Let's allow me to feel my experience fully, and ask all the questions that pour out, and grasp for incomplete answers that seem to satisfy for a moment. Let's agree that what I'm experiencing is real and overwhelming (at least to me, right now). Let's trust that I won't feel this way forever, and that I'll come back to you at a later date to hear more about your challenges and the ways in which you've coped. Let's simply sit in silence, if necessary, and feel what it is to be human, in all of its confusion and fear.

Relief

The night after the day Will died was unbearably painful, lonely, and dramatic. (Just as in the movies, I indulged in the whole scream-at-God-into-the-night-sky cliché and everything.) At the same time—and to be perfectly honest—it was also the soundest sleep I'd enjoyed in the months before or since. No more alarms to listen for, no more dragging myself out of bed at 3 a.m., no more obsessive bottle washing, no more sterilizing breast-pump parts, no more warming of milk and careful measurement of supplements, no more tedious sending of a tiny air bubble down his feeding tube to check it for proper placement at each and every feed, no more parceling out each 24 hours into 3-hour increments (which were between 9 a.m. and 9 p.m. anyway—actually half-hour preps for feeds, 30-minute feeds, 30-minute interactions, 15-minute nap inducements, 10-minute cleanup, plus diapers and crying and vomit and rashes and all of that other normal baby stuff). No more standing over his bed in the middle of the night, trying to remember if he was on his left shoulder or right shoulder at midnight, and so where should I leave him now? Of course, he has better digestion when lying on his left side, so that's important. But he can't always lie on that side, so do I take a chance with vomit/reflux now, or should I play it safe for digestion?

No more refrigerated and non-refrigerated meds, dosed out in syringes in increments down to .05 milliliters (and you'd better not mix up this flight of meds and give him an antacid-sized dose of his heart med, or go blank on whether you gave him his 6 o'clock meds that morning . . . or was it yesterday?). No more checking the calendar on the computer to discover that, oh yeah, today is Thursday and we need to go to the outpatient clinic this afternoon for another cardiac ultrasound, and the feeding team is coming for a home visit in an hour, and I'd better call the home health nurse to remind her not to come, since he'll be weighed and measured at the clinic. No more worries about finding special schools and feeling the constraints of having to live close to medical care and developmental experts. No more long, slow draining of our savings while bankruptcy looms on the horizon.

The guilt over our sense of relief was multiplied in the month following the funeral. Once our family members went back home and our friends returned to their lives, we took advantage of our newfound freedom and did a little traveling. Nothing too dramatic—a six-hour drive to the beach in North Carolina, a last-minute trip to a regular gathering of friends in New Mexico, followed by a week staying with friends in the San Francisco Bay Area—but opportunities we'd never have experienced had our son been alive. Indeed, even upon our return home, mundane things like going to the grocery store or outlet mall or park would give us a pang of guilt as we realized we had given up such luxuries when we joined our lives with Will's. We had sacrificed all of this freedom, and getting it back only made us feel worse.

This relief and freedom has a dark side, particularly for those who find themselves in similar situations. Even now, we have a few friends with special-needs kids with whom we share an almost wordless understanding that although our hearts are broken—and theirs with ours—there is a real sense that we have gotten off easy. While they continue on with their steadfast, sacrificial care of their children, we find ourselves at the end of that difficult road, and not by our own choosing.

We've traded the long, slow grind of a lifetime of days doled out in the service of another for a short, intense experience of pain. Sure, we suffer now, but we also don't need to make any more appointments, don't have to schedule any more surgeries, don't have to wonder if that person in the elevator is staring at our child out of admiration or pity or revulsion. We don't need to worry over the best method of telling our child that his heart has an expiration date, and that we'll probably need to start looking for another one sometime before he turns thirty. We don't need to help him decide if he should attend college or marry or have children with such deep uncertainty ahead. We don't need to explain, over and over, why his sister can run and he can't, why he can't learn to surf, why he'll never be "normal." Grief is brutal, but it is at least final.

I think about all the time and money and non-biodegradable medical waste dedicated to this one life. Every time I do so, I conclude that it was a high price, yes, but it was worth it for us to know our son. It was worth it for others to know him, and to love him, and to receive his love. And besides, how can we put a price on human life, and what kind of society would this become if human worth were graded on a curve?

I always come to this confident conclusion while at the same time feeling fairly certain that I'd not mention such reasoning to a mother in Africa who had just lost her baby with hypoplastic left heart syndrome (HLHS) at three days of life, or to the mother next to her whose child is starving. Those lives are not worth any less, but they are not valued nearly as much, at least by those of us on *this* side of the planet. Our family's medical insurance (thank God for such a thing!) paid out over $800,000 in expenses, and that was only for the first surgery. Will would have had at least two more open-heart surgeries, plus at least three facial surgeries, plus recovery from all of that, plus constant ongoing care. The numbers are staggering, especially when one considers how far such funds would go in other parts of the world, and all the people who would be helped.

Was it worth it? I can't say. Or maybe I'm simply afraid to say it out loud. But I know this: when I recently heard about a pregnant woman who chose to terminate her HLHS baby at five months' gestation, I simultaneously condemned her as a heartless and selfish ogre while at the same time I understood, to some degree, why she wanted to make that choice. And I cried at the horror of those painful choices we both made.

Optimistic

It's difficult to look back and remember. Not only because of the pain and loss and heartache but because of the hope and the optimism we felt.

I remember the innumerable times I walked through an ICU entryway, paused to wash my hands, and then went to his bedside. Every single time, seeing or hearing some report of encouraging news mixed with some bit of bad news. Every single time, seeing a child where he should not be: staring up at lights, connected to tubes, confined to a bed, being *here* when he should be *home*. And every single time I took all this in and blindly chose to hope for the best outcome in the shortest amount of time.

I look at photos now, and cringe. In them I see a tiny, sickly baby bristling with medical equipment, staring at the camera with an unexpected intelligence and a kind of weighty consideration of his environment. And I see his father, eyes bright, face fresh, and with a big, dumb grin. How could I have been so happy? How could I have been so inured to his life and limits? How could I have turned such a blind eye to the simple reality right in front of me?

I look at the artifacts of those days together—of the journal entries, poems, and blog posts—and am chagrined at my optimism, embarrassed by my stubborn hope. I used to get up every morning at 3 a.m. to give him a tube feeding. I'd wake to an alarm, tiptoe by his bed, warm the breast milk and fortify it with formula, and quietly set up the pump that would deliver the food so as not to wake him. In the twenty or thirty minutes of waiting that followed, I would often hammer out goofy blog posts. Reading them now, they look celebratory—prideful, even—and I recoil in shame. How could I know that my time with him would be so limited? How could I not? Why didn't I sit with him, or pray for him, or write to him, instead of exploiting my own sleep deprivation in a feeble attempt at humor?

As I write this, I'm seeing all this from the perspective of yet another gut-wrenching, emotionally withering, physically exhausting episode in the life of our little church. It is a situation familiar to anyone who joins their life with others in an effort to live after God: heartbreak, pain both felt and dealt, silent struggles for power, utter confusion, and clumsy attempts at love and reconciliation. None of this misery, of course, is willful or even conscious. But it is all real, nevertheless.

We are, all of us, broken vessels of God's goodness, trying our best to work together to bring God's kingdom. We are, all of us, choosing to hope and offer grace, instead of retreating to abject cynicism. One friend who has been through situations like this many times before has offered this bleak (but not unhopeful) outlook: "It's not this situation that is so difficult—it is knowing that this will settle out, that God will come through, that we'll help each other to the best outcome possible. The painful part is knowing that we'll go through stuff like this again and again."

Isn't that life? Don't we all need to choose every day to commit ourselves completely to the cause—whatever it may be—and give it our all? To lead with our heart and believe the best, and deny disappointment, and to shrug off cynicism in favor of a kind of determined innocence, a childlike faith? Jesus said we should be wise as serpents and, at the same time, innocent as doves. Living wholeheartedly will involve peace and pain in turn.

Living like this is, it seems to me, the only way. If I can be permitted a false dichotomy, I would submit that the alternative is to live in the drab, gray world of halfhearted commitment, stingy love, measured passions, and false hope. When I was a child, my parents taught me that if I had low expectations, I'd be pleasantly surprised by good outcomes. While the truth of this is undeniable, it seems rather bleak as well. I wonder what I've missed when I've followed this (solid) logic.

I used to run every day. It was good exercise and a nice relief from the grind of life. I'd finish my runs feeling fresh and slightly euphoric, happy to be outside and active and glad to feel the tingling of my body's electrical impulses. Running is a great escape and a worthy enterprise in itself. Many people do it nearly every day in a kind of solitary pursuit. But until you lace up your shoes, pin on a race number, and toe the starting line, you'll never know how slow or fast you really are. You'll never know how good it feels to go fast or how much it hurts to really push yourself. You'll never know the elation of a new personal best or the disappointment of a flat performance. To my mind, it is better to live on the ragged edge than to engage in risk-free adventure and a pain-free existence. At least then you know you're alive. For isn't pain a part of life?

Living like this may be the best way, but it hurts. A lot. Hold back, and stay safe, and you'll be okay. Life will be comfortable and measured and predictable, if a little bland.

But range to the edge of things and you'll feel the heat and the cold, the pleasure and pain, the exhilaration and disappointment of the life that lies beyond the bounds of safety and security. The life that takes one beyond the ready comforts, even, of God. It is Jesus himself who challenges us to sacrifice ourselves and our pursuits to love the Other. That isn't easy, or pain-free. For it was Jesus who said the words, "My God, my God, why have you forsaken me?"

Spring

As winter loosens its grip, it ushers in a season of green, of hope, and of frozen ground thawing into new life. Rhythms of life change, and even the liturgical calendars of most faith traditions reflect the shifting season. Simplistic though it feels, the breaking of spring is somehow reflected in my general mood and disposition. I'm not sure if it's the literal, physical growth in the gardens that I tend, or the books I've been reading, or the folks I've been hanging out with, or the baptism of our girl, or the sun that shines more now, or the developmental milestones of Eleanor. Or maybe it's just the passing of time, or a passing mood. All I know is that I feel lighter and that I'll take what I can get.

Walking through the yard with my daughter in the early spring, it is hopeful indeed to notice buds on the trees and bushes—new life bursting forth. As we pause under the towering oak tree in the backyard, I see the grass I planted when my wife was pregnant one year ago. I remember how I prepared the soil and carefully scattered and covered the seeds with fresh dirt and pieces of straw to hold the soil and thwart the birds, and how I watered it diligently. I did what I could, but I honestly didn't expect much in the way of growth. Here under the tree, the existing grass is spare and spotty as it fights for life and light under a large canopy of acidic leaves. Life is not easy, and I didn't want to get my hopes up.

But grow it did. Not everywhere, and not overwhelmingly, but it grew nonetheless. In spite of my doubts, those tiny seeds sent up the purest, greenest shoots, filling in the bare spots and filling me with hope. I remember this because, even a year later, the little patches peeked up with delicate strands of grass that were several shades lighter than the surrounding lawn. Which might have reminded me of my disappointment, but which gave me hope all over again, somehow.

At the same time, spring also brings death. Or rather the fresh growth on the larger plants shows by contrast the branches that didn't survive the winter. So I move among the green branches, reaching into the bushes and trees to carefully follow the dry dead branches all the way back to their origin, and cutting just past these supple green signs of life. My hands move automatically as I relieve the plant of these dead pieces and allow more light to pass into and through the plant. The dead branches snap when they are squeezed with the pruning shears, and they are light and brittle as I toss them into the trash can by my side. Throwing away the dead bits could be depressing, but it frees my mind to let go of dead thoughts, unhealthy coping mechanisms, dead-ended ideas, unrealistic fantasies, and other unhelpful pieces of my psyche.

The spring-cleaning happens indoors too, as we go through papers and books and toys to get rid of what we can, and to organize everything else. We pull articles of summer clothing from boxes, swapping their places on shelves and hangers and drawers with their counterparts, filling the boxes instead with the dark, heavy clothes of winter. As we do so, we keep a sharp eye out for clothes and shoes we no longer use, setting them aside to give to charity. In the same way, we sort through the wardrobe of our rapidly growing girl, filling a container with cute clothes that no longer fit. In the limited confines of our apartment, if something is not paying its freight, then there's no point in keeping it around. Though we'd rather she not grow up at all, we dutifully separate the pieces too small for her and stock her drawers with pieces that will allow her to grow.

Digging into storage reveals painful things, too. When Will died, we filled crates with paperwork, medical supplies, newspaper eulogies, toys, blankets, special clothing, and other reminders of our days together. We've put these precious things away, hoping that someday soon we'll have the strength to sort through these painful reminders and decide what we must keep and what we should give to someone else.

As I crawled to the very back of our deepest storage cubby with a flashlight to survey the boxes of painful memories, my wife summoned me with the news that our daughter was taking her first steps. Emerging from the closet, I looked into the kitchen, where our girl had taken advantage of our inattention to rise to her feet, let go of the shelf next to her to begin taking small but sure steps toward us. We shouted encouragement and squealed with glee while she stared back at us in disbelief, as if to say, What's the big deal? She walked slowly for several minutes, catching her tiny sways and correcting her course in admirable fashion.

Standing there on my own two feet, watching her standing there on her own two feet, it occurred to me that life, growth, and healing can simply happen, even apart from our intentionality and attention. Quite often, in spite of it. Perhaps that's the most beautiful element of spring.

Baptism Poems

In April, we held a church service where we baptized Eleanor. William was heavy on our minds that day, since this was originally intended to be a baptism for both of them, held on the weekend that ended up being the time when we held his funeral.

I was ruminating on the interconnectedness they enjoyed a year earlier as they were both in utero. About how Will's placenta was insufficiently attached to his mother's cervix, yet how his survival was necessary for his sister's. And about how, when they were delivered, we were astounded to learn that his placenta had attached to hers so that they were giving each other life.

Losing My Will; Finding My Way

I want to remember
I want to remember
I want to remember
This three-pound person
Who gave us light
And gave us life
He gave us Eleanor
Placenta clinging to uterus
drawing sustenance
Through a tiny thread
He survived
He persevered
No
He triumphed
and brought us to this day

I want to remember
I want to remember
I want to remember
Not pain
Not regret
Not guilt
No

I want to remember
His head on my shoulder
Utter Joy
Wide smiles
Gentle cooing
Loud screaming
Rigid muscles resisting mine
A spirit unbroken

I want to be thankful
For Will
I want to have
More will
To go on
To live on
To retain my memory
And
To release my grip
And
To travel with Eleanor Elisabeth and Stacy Ann
On the road to Galilee

I want to remember
I want to remember
I want to remember
That there is a Way
A way to live
A way of life
A way that leads to real life
Blessed are the poor
Blessed are those who mourn
Blessed are the meek
Though he slay me
I'm gonna keep on walkin',
Keep on talkin',
Marchin' up to freedom land

My Dearest Eleanor

Today I offer you myself
Not the me that I am
But the me that I will become
The new me that will join with the new you
As we learn about the world together
The world that is seen
And the greater world that is unseen
That underlying, overlaid presence that permeates
    this place
Everywhere and nowhere, all at once
Like daylilies pushing up through the soil
Like aimless birds with plenty to eat
Like a warm breeze beckoning
Like a mountain spring flowing
Enough for us both
to cleanse and sustain and refresh
the pure, clear waters of grace

So let's walk the path together
You show me and I'll show you
To live in the here and now
To live the now and then
With eyes to see
One world being undone by another
And to be undone ourselves

We named you "light," and you are
A bright beam that cuts through my fog
With you, I am undone by love
It is
A divine conspiracy
A holy subversion
A quiet kingdom come

By chance, a friend from California, Mark Scandrette, was
in town with his family, and they joined us. During the time

of prayer and sharing that was a part of Eleanor's baptism service, Mark read out loud his poem "Ella Elisabeth."

Ella Elisabeth
Who through force of Will
Now graces us
With her presence
May you grow in wisdom
And in stature
And in favor
With God and people
May the seed of the Maker's good dreams
Leap and sprout inside of you
Nurturing you to become
The woman you were made to be

Itsy-Bitsy Spider

Many people suffering a loss like mine, or the grief that follows it, or the mild depression that hangs over one's head, would likely have a difficult time getting out of bed in the morning. Questions swirl around our sleepy heads.

Why should I go on?

What should I do?

What could be worthy of my effort when so much has been taken from me?

I don't have that option. Before I can even get philosophical in the morning, I face a very pragmatic call to action: the grinning face of my daughter and her whole-arm wave as I pry open my eyes. Before I can even think about it, I get up bright and early every single morning—simply because she needs me to. She is up and awake, eager to share a full diaper of one kind or the other, and to find something to quell the pang in her stomach, and to satisfy the look of mischief on her dimpled face.

Now, there is nothing heroic about my service to her. I force myself to smile back at her, and groan as I move my middle-aged bones out of bed and wordlessly carry her to the kitchen. There, she graciously allows me to pursue Priority Number One each day: Coffee. Standing in her playpen, she watches me heat the water and ready the pot. She tracks the beans as they move from cupboard to coffee grinder, then sings along as it makes its monotonous music. She watches me as I stare at the water, willing it to boil. Finally, she sees the cloud of steam when ground coffee meets hot water and the lid goes on the pot. Sometimes, as we're waiting for the magic to happen, she'll grow anxious. Some petulant whining, or perhaps shouts of protest will leave her mouth. Coffee's spell is temporarily broken and she loses her composure.

At which point I will bust out my secret weapon: a simple song that includes pantomime and drama, tragedy and triumph, hardship and resolution. She might not understand the words, but she seems to enjoy my dancing around the kitchen as I tell the age-old story:

> The itsy-bitsy spider
> Crawled up the water spout.
> Down came the rain
> And washed the spider out.
> Out came the sun
> And dried up all the rain.
> And the itsy-bitsy spider
> Crawled up the spout again.

It usually requires a couple of repetitions, but eventually, like the rain, her tears are chased away by my sunny-faced recitation, and we can move toward the time when she finally gets her breakfast.

I know that someday, when she's older, this little remedy will lose its effectiveness. By sheer repetition she'll grow bored of my little trick. Moreover, I've peeked ahead in the parenting books and know there will be an epoch of her life when questions will be the center of our conversations. When the "Why?" will be thrown down at every opportunity, and I'll be scrambling for age-appropriate explanations.

And I wonder what *whys* she might ask of this story. Why did the spider crawl up the spout? Why did the rain come? Why did the sun come?

And with my proclivity toward theology, I wonder, will I break out the God-talk? Will I say, "God brings the rain," and try to expand on the goodness of rain to minimize its disorienting and displacing effects on our friend the spider? If enough farmers and food-eaters get a benefit from the rain, does that offset the detrimental effect of the rain on the spiders and playground-goers of the world? How can we balance these scales?

Will I say, "God brings the sun," and talk about how God is the source of all goodness in the world, and that God wants to help the spider by drying out our poor friend's home? In which case she should rightly ask *why* the rain comes back, just as it does as I repeat the song again and again. (If she asks why the spider lives in a downspout, will I rail about systemic injustice in the world, including homelessness, human trafficking, and economic disparity?) How can we balance the equation?

Or will I follow the lead of some parents and theologians and split the equation? Will I say the rain is in fact bad, but that God brings the sun? Will I engage in some fiery flourish of fundamentalism and suggest that the devil sends the rain but God brings the sun (and that someday The Son will Reign over the Devil!). Or will I speak as some preachers: God brings the rain as the punishment we all deserve, and God brings sun as pure mercy (since we all deserve eternal punishment). And we'd better be good, and we'd better be thankful for the sun, or we'll get even more rain (which we deserve!).

At which point I imagine my incessantly questioning girl will ask a few more questions, pointing out that the rain and the sun each possess both positive and negative traits: they work together to bring beautiful flowers, green grass, and Christmas trees. Too much of one means drought and melanoma, and too much of the other means flooding and soggy spiders with eight wet feet.

Philosophers and theologians have had a lot of time to ask "Why?" and so have developed theories and philosophical constructs. The one that the poor spider might cite is often referred to as "theodicy." This concept attempts to resolve a tension: If God is good, and if God is powerful, then how do we account for all the pain and suffering in the world? How do we balance the scales between God's omnipotence on the one side, and human agency on the other? How do we make peace with the pain in the world?

Since 1710, when Gottfried Leibniz coined the term *theodicy*, those who think about God and yet who live in this world of pain have tinkered with these ideas and suggested ways to relieve the tension. Some have said that God doesn't exist. Others have suggested God's goodness or power may be muted in some ways, or brokered or mediated imperfectly such that the fullness of these realities isn't evident to human reasoning.

In his book *The Weakness of God*, John Caputo boldly suggests that God is good, but God is in fact "not all-powerful," or at least not powerful in the way we might like. To the spider, and to my daughter, I imagine Caputo bending down, smiling, and saying that both the rain and the sun *just happen*. It's not exactly fair to assign blame or to praise God for every little thing that happens in this great big world. Using his terms (borrowed from physics), God uses not a *strong force*, but a *weak force*.

Perhaps the most helpful example of these many weak forces is gravity, something that's a complete mystery yet holds our entire world, solar system, galaxy, and universe together. This minute attraction of one particle to another is a tiny force, but it's enough to enable life as we know it. Like the way of God, gravity is broad, distributed, and pervasive. Weak and strong at the same time.

So instead of picturing God as a giant with his sleeves rolled up, only occasionally reaching down to move and shape the world, we might better view God as exercising an underlying, pervasive kind of strength that brings goodness from the bottom up. In this conception, God is just as big (maybe bigger!) and just as powerful (maybe more powerful!) because God is active throughout the universe, rather than contained in any one realm. We live in, and walk through, a God-soaked world that is being inexorably reshaped and reborn into the fullness of God. God is not sitting on some regal throne, commanding us to be meek because we are so pitiful. God is in the mix, showing us *how* to be meek (which is much different from being weak or ineffectual). God is not passive-aggressively repressing anger at humanity until the day when God is finally able to punish us. God is working in and amongst humanity to redeem all things.

This adds new freshness to passages like 2 Corinthians 12:

> I must go on boasting. Although there is nothing to be gained, I will go on to visions and revelations from the Lord. I know a man in Christ who fourteen years ago was caught up to the third heaven. Whether it was in the body or out of the body I do not know—God knows. And I know that this

man—whether in the body or apart from the body I do not know, but God knows—was caught up to paradise and heard inexpressible things, things that no one is permitted to tell. I will boast about a man like that, but I will not boast about myself, except about my weaknesses. Even if I should choose to boast, I would not be a fool, because I would be speaking the truth. But I refrain, so no one will think more of me than is warranted by what I do or say, or because of these surpassingly great revelations. Therefore, in order to keep me from becoming conceited, I was given a thorn in my flesh, a messenger of Satan, to torment me. Three times I pleaded with the Lord to take it away from me. But he said to me, "My grace is sufficient for you, for my power is made perfect in weakness." Therefore I will boast all the more gladly about my weaknesses, so that Christ's power may rest on me. That is why, for Christ's sake, I delight in weaknesses, in insults, in hardships, in persecutions, in difficulties. For when I am weak, then I am strong.

2 Corinthians 12:1–10

So it is strength, yes. But it is a different kind of strength. Broad rather than localized. Diffused rather than focused. Unexpected rather than predictable. Pervasive but not always recognizable.

I've seen God accomplish things I can only characterize as miracles: instantaneous healings, inexplicable insights, and displays of divine energy in ordinary human bodies. Indeed, my second marathon was one I ran on a knee that just forty-eight hours before wouldn't allow me even to walk on it. My friend Dave prayed for my knee, and the next morning it was working fine. In the ten years and four marathons since, it hasn't even had a hitch. But if we are waiting for God to reach down and fix everything, we're going to be tired, frustrated, and dead. And if we blame God for everything that goes wrong—hurricanes, earthquakes, illness, and untimely death—then we turn

God into a capricious monster. God's power is real, though it undergirds us more than it overpowers us.

Doesn't Jesus suggest as much? In our accounts of Jesus' teaching, we learn of tiny seeds that grow into huge plants, and of invaluable treasures that crop up in the most unexpected places. He declares what would appear to be economic nonsense about leaving ninety-nine sheep to pursue a solitary lamb, and about a father ignoring his loyal, dutiful son to wait in agonized vigil for his hell-raising, rebellious boy. He talks about daylilies that enjoy and provide unspeakable splendor, and about ubiquitous birds that somehow always find something to eat. Which might seem inconsequential in our world of fusion and genetic engineering and cloning, but I ask you: Can we in all of our ingenuity create a flower or a tiny bird? Can we count them all? Can we even calculate the required resources and organization involved with feeding and growing all the lilies and sparrows in the world?

Jesus describes a kingdom, but it is not what the early followers expect it to be. They expect Jesus to grab the reins of power and lead a rebellion, and he provides the ultimate disappointment—an embarrassing and ignominious death on a cross. No, Jesus' kingdom is one of daylilies and sparrows, of widows and orphans, of the meek and the mourners: the powerless overcoming the powerful forces set against them, even if it takes millennia for the whole system to be overturned, one pebble at a time.

Not that we can blame these early Christians for their confusion. After all, there were times when Jesus' arm was very strong indeed. Jesus reached out and healed people's lifelong ailments. The blind saw, the lame walked, the oppressed were set free, the dead emerged out of tombs. Make no mistake, these were experiences of power—of God powerfully breaking in and changing things. But at the same time, these things happened to powerless people (and they didn't happen to many other people, whether powerless or powerful). Too, though they were healed, they like birds and lilies eventually died.

Jesus' own experience is instructive here as well. In his powerful book *The Crucified God*, Jürgen Moltmann poses the fascinating question, "What did the cross mean *for God?*" It meant an eternal ability to identify with those who suffer loss, among many other things. Jesus knows what it is like to experience God's absence. And God feels sorrow and pain and is in fact a figure of great suffering. But God is also a source of great joy and hope, for God is one who has seen goodness wrought from pain since time out of mind.

I had the privilege of meeting John Caputo a few months after our son died. We greeted each other in the hallway following his philosophy conference that I had attended. My wife was there too, so I introduced Dr. Caputo to her and to my daughter, and thanked him for his work. I started to tell him our story of loss, and he kindly interrupted me. Looking into my eyes and opening his hands, he said, "How are you doing?" Utterly sincere, he patiently listened as my wife and I tried to summarize. Eager to get the conversation back on track (and to allow him to move along), I thanked him for his books and said they had helped me greatly as I struggled with the question, "How could God let this happen?"

He stopped me again as he gave me the kindest smile, nodded, and said, "I think that is the wrong question."

I look out the window today and see the rain fall. Spiders hunker under leaves, little girls have to wear hats, and bedraggled teachers and caregivers need to entertain children indoors. But I also realize that same rain nourishes the flowers outside my window and creates the stunning palisades surrounding the Potomac River at Great Falls, where I walked yesterday, and the Grand Canyon in the American West, where I was overwhelmed several years ago. It's just rain, yes, but it's powerful when it is consistent and pervasive.

I look out the window and think of my son. I miss him, of course, and would give anything to share another day with him, whether sunny or rainy. One would expect that thinking about a meek God would foster negativity, hopelessness, nihilism. But somehow, deconstructing my expectations of God creates hope and optimism. Adjusting my expectations of God's interventions, and of the nature of God's work in the world, mollifies my anger at him for not reaching down to change our fortunes. It helps me make sense of Will's short life—a life that, all at once, evidenced both strength and weakness. And it gives me strength, even if it is only the strength of daylilies.

Birthday Party

On a day of mixed emotions, we took our daughter to a local petting zoo for the celebration of her first birthday. Along with her friends and their parents, it was wonderful to witness the variety of creatures and to see the excitement of the interactions between animals and kids. At the same time I was the stereotypical dad with checklists coursing through my head, and maps, toys, tickets, and pacifiers bulging out of my many pockets. And after all the animals had been fed and the ponies had been ridden and the snacks and cake had been consumed and everyone was washing their hands and giving a final good-bye to the goats, I went back to police the trash from our picnic area and pick up the last of the party supplies and carry the cooler to the car.

In the quiet vacuum left behind by the absence of kids and parents and talking birds, I felt especially lonely. I thought of my son, who shares this same birthday, and who I desperately wished could be here. And I cried for a minute, happy for the catharsis and empowered to rejoin my friends.

Expectations

I'm fortunate to know two first grade teachers. One is my sister Pamela, who faithfully teaches at the very elementary school she attended as a kid. Beautiful, brilliant, and generous, she is the kind of teacher every parent covets for their child. The other is my close friend Jackie, who manages to juggle several balls each day: a roomful of seven-year-olds, a demanding graduate school program, significant social engagement with family, church, and friends, and a very creative new husband who is himself busily juggling at least five artistic/business ventures at any one time. I love knowing them both, and seeing the world through their eyes.

First grade intrigues me because it seems to be the start of so much. Early socialization, a new kind of independence, and the beginnings of formal left-brain development with skills like simple math. But most interesting to me is the wondrous world of reading.

On the first day of school, after introducing herself to her new class who shine in their first-day finery, flush with pristine school supplies, my sister will lower her voice, scan the sea of anxious eyes before her, smile her perfect smile, and give a well-rehearsed little speech.

"This year I will teach you to read. Some of you can already do it a little, and some of you are pretty scared about it. But I promise that we'll work together, and by the end of the school year we'll all be able to read."

And they do. With her credentials as a reading specialist, and her natural gifts of nurture and empowerment, Pamela will have each and every one of those kids reading far above their grade level in nine short months. Can you imagine anything more wondrous, intimidating, or important? Reading opens a whole world to us—a key that unlocks almost everything else. I myself remember sitting in Mrs. Otto's first grade class, flush with the excitement of reading and writing for myself, and yet looking around for a minute to realize that the boys and girls around me who were struggling would probably continue to do so. Each of us was setting a trajectory for our next fifteen or so years in the classroom, and our lives thereafter. First grade, I thought to my tiny self, is the most important year of our lives, and I felt the great weight of my personal responsibility to learn.

Jackie is a great teacher, too (though genetics and family pride force me to speak more readily of my sister). One of the classroom projects she told me about hit me right between the eyes, causing me to think that perhaps reading isn't the most important thing in life.

It is spring as I write this, and Jackie is currently teaching her class about seeds, and growth, and expectations. Not by standing in front of a board or by reading them a book—no, her class is learning from experience, for better and for worse. They're planting seeds in pots of dirt, watering them, and waiting for them to grow. Which sounds like a messy, wonderfully exciting project for teacher and student alike. And it sounds like a fun one too, as she describes wide-eyed kids jumping up from their seats after only an hour to run to the windowsill to see what progress has been made.

But reality is not so cute. Just as in reading and math, some students feel the ecstasy of success, while others experience the bitter taste of failure. After first realizing that agricultural progress is generally measured in days and weeks, rather than hours, the wide-eyed students learn even harder lessons about life. For most, their antsy patience is rewarded with a shoot of green, then a stalk, then a beautiful flower—a touch of grace, an indescribable miracle, a joyful celebration of a new kind of magic. But for others, the waiting leads to more waiting, and then more. Some seeds rot in the soil even as the pots around them burst with life. Some soil remains unmoved while the big blooms in the next pot cast shadows across its surface. Children watch their classmates celebrate and try to face their own disappointment.

What can you tell a little kid to comfort them? How can you answer their questions? How can you ease their pain and disappointment? Jackie tries to explain that some seeds get too much water while others get too little. Some seeds grow, and others don't. She tries to counsel them about life—to share their pain and disappointment without fostering cynicism or a bleak outlook, and to help them hang on to hope. She tries to help them understand that none of this is their fault. Each child had the best of intentions and applied their skills as best they could, but things just didn't work out. It's nobody's fault. That's just life. Even as they experience the thrill of new friendships, growth, and learning during one of the very best years of their lives, they learn that things don't always turn out the way we'd like. All of their yearnings won't change that.

It's a harsh lesson, to be sure. Life and death coexist. Success is tempered by disappointment. Sometimes we see success, and other times we suffer failure. Sometimes this is our fault, yet most of the time it's just the way things work out. Sad, but true. Harsh, but honest. Bitter, but real.

Life sometimes fails to flourish. Maybe that's the best lesson we can learn—the earlier, the better. It is, I think, the first step toward hope. Without it, we rail against our neighbors, stew in doubt and self-hatred, harbor jealousy, and ask "Why?" when—understandable and honest as that question is—it's a question without a real answer.

On Ants

It's part selfishness and part self-therapy that brings us back to the children's hospital again and again.

Selfish, because the brilliant pediatrician who became a dear friend is still there, and we can't imagine a better person to care for our daughter—or indeed for our entire family. Shortly after he bitterly wept over Will's body and attended the funeral, not as a crisp professional but as a sorrowful and broken man, he ran a marathon in Will's honor, wearing a handmade T-shirt emblazoned with his name. He invited me to join him for the middle miles on the section of the course that is my favorite part of DC. So, though it is a longish drive to that hospital, and though we need to pay for parking, we can't imagine going to a pediatrician closer to our home.

The path to the hospital is so familiar that the car seems to drive itself, and we ride in relative silence. It's like traveling through a time tunnel as my wife and I offer disjointed commentary and asynchronous remembrances as we follow the same route, wait at the same traffic lights, and search for a spot in the same garage. We don't need to take the elevators anymore, since there are only three of us, and we no longer need to push a stroller laden with bags and supplies, but we usually take the elevator anyway. It is not easy, this walking in our old footsteps, but it seems a good—if harsh—way to remember and heal. It feels a little like redemption.

Once we've completed our visit in the pediatric clinic, we always make our way to the main part of the building. We usually don't visit the second-floor cardiac ICU where Will was first admitted. It is at the end of a long hall, which makes our lurking there seem especially obvious and sad and desperate. We avoid that place, and the other ICUs where we spent so much time, but we do head up to the third floor and pass through the heart and kidney unit to the tiny office of our social worker. The unit is laid out in a loop such that we could either follow one route directly to her door, or another that would pass by the room where Will died, along with another room where he spent the whirlwind week before we were shuttled off to an acute-care facility up the road. I can only think of one instance that we didn't take the more painful route, and where I didn't pause in front of The Room.

Sometimes The Room is empty, which seems good and right . . . holy, even. There's no noise in there, no worry, no family wailing around a pale body on the bed while a tiny baby coos and cries in the corner. At other times, there is a patient in there, and I am forced to perform a more socially acceptable glance over the room—to look and not appear to be *looking* so as not to intrude. When the room holds a patient, it's easy to feel displaced and to grieve not only our loss but the fact that another child and family are going through a very difficult time. At the same time it feels good and redemptive to hope for a better outcome for them, and to recognize that life goes on. In any case, I always pause for a second or two and feel progressively lighter each time I do so.

When we visited the hospital yesterday, the low patient census in the cardiac unit meant that both our social worker and her colleague were in their office, and we all had a nice time celebrating our girl as she toddled around in the hall as we talked about our adjustment to life. My brain quickly hits overdrive in such situations, massively overthinking the innocent questions posed to me, such as "How are you?" and "How is work?" But these kind professionals are patient and gracious and help me to relax and to talk about what I'd like, in the way that I'd like.

I also overthink the legacy of Will that our social worker often mentions; the ways in which she is reminded of him. The overactive part of my brain doubts that he could possibly stand out amongst her many patients and wonders if she is exaggerating his influence, even as the more stable part of my brain banks on her utter sincerity and kindness. Or maybe it's the simple fact that if she's misleading me, I'm happy to be misled and to have Will's memory honored so. I quiet my brain and remember that I'm among friends.

Of course, there's a dark side to this memory, and she reflected that, until recently, she had always considered the room at the end of the hall to be "Will's Room," moved as she was by his death, and engaged as she was in our grief on that dark Tuesday morning where the sun shone in a most unkind way, and where she patiently guided us through the long process of accepting the reality before us and walking away from his body. On that morning it became Will's Room and stayed that way for months, until a few weeks ago, when the presence of some pesky insects transformed it into "The Ant Room."

She told us the humorous story of noticing the problem during a tense meeting between several doctors and a family, and how she had made arrangements for the family to be moved to more hospitable environs. I'm sure the problem has been rectified (in a way that is pleasant for both people and ants), and that the room is back in use. And I realize I might well be bitter that a place so significant has become—for her, and now for me—so inauspicious. That its moniker has moved from that of a beloved person to a colony of irritating insects. But somehow, and for some reason hard to describe, I'm happy for the change, and ready for the room and for myself to move on, and for the pain to subside instead of echoing endlessly.

Hitting the Wall

Unwinding the Spring

If the winter last year was about waiting and hoping, then the spring was a breakneck race through a series of life-altering events that rushed at us in an insane jumble. Once the twins were born, the pace of our lives ramped up to a breathless rush of impossible decisions, unspeakable disappointments, and the sense that we were being pulled along considerably faster than our feet would move. It all happened so fast that we're only now putting it all together, reliving those days last year, stopping occasionally to hit "pause" on our thoughts so we can try to make sense of them.

During their first few days of life, our hope was that we would be able to keep Will in the ICU of the hospital where they were born, close to his mother as she recovered. Unfortunately, within hours of his birth, his breathing became ineffective and so we were forced to have him transported to the children's hospital across town, where his surgery would take place. With our family split up this way, I would spend the night in the hospital room of my wife and daughter, then hurry across town to spend the day at the other hospital with Will and his medical team.

I thought this separation of mother and child would be a relief for my wife: that I was sparing her the pain of seeing our boy on a ventilator, uncomfortable and laid out in a tiny bed. However, she was desperate to see him, and so only two days after giving birth she literally sneaked out of the hospital and I reluctantly drove her across town to the children's hospital.

She shuffled to the side of his bed, still feeling the pain of a fresh C-section. I stood behind to catch her if her knees gave out. What happened was made even more striking from my limited vantage point. Cut off from her visage and looking only at her back, neck, and shoulders I saw her face turn toward his while her muscles tensed, then relaxed slightly. To my utter surprise she stood up straighter, stronger, more whole. In their reunion, a circuit had been closed and a flow of love and energy that had been interrupted was once again complete. It was I who was undone in the face of such a display of a mother's love and care, I whose knees went weak, and I who stepped back to collapse into a chair.

The next morning all of the assembled family visited Will before the six-hour surgery that would reroute the vessels around his heart to allow the two right chambers of the heart to supply blood to his organs, leaving the return flow between the lungs and heart to operate passively. The most disconcerting part of the surgery would involve the use of ice to chill his body, inducing hypothermia to reduce the extent of any damage to his brain while the flow of his blood and his heart were stopped for the most critical connections to be made. Each of us tried to find some way to offer him our prayers and best wishes, along with some kind of good-bye before the anesthesiologists came to roll his tiny bed to the operating room.

My wife and I grabbed a little lunch and then promptly headed down to the pediatric clinic to have the experts there evaluate the rapid weight loss of our daughter and her progressing case of jaundice, along with other concerns about her spine and kidneys. Looking back, it seems cruel to have been so encumbered by such a worrisome task, but at the time it felt like a relief to be distracted with serious but less than life-threatening health concerns. These worries threatened to push us over the edge, but they were at least controllable conditions that we had some hope of fixing. Upstairs, we were helpless. Upstairs, we could only worry, and what would that help? So we assessed Eleanor and made plans to return to have her weighed every other day until further notice. In the process I had my first chance to change one of her poopy diapers, my inexperience evident to the watchful nurse who patiently waited for me to finish, and who wordlessly forgave my inattention to the sign that hung in front of my face demanding that diapers be changed in the restroom only.

The hours in the clinic passed quickly. We returned to the waiting room to see our family, all of whom were huddled around a beeper meant to receive text messages, updating us on the surgery's progress, which we later learned wasn't working that day. Still, we received verbal updates as the stages of the surgery were completed, and one especially weighty update that the sixty-minute absolute deadline for the hypothermic "complete arrest" was met, by one minute. Finally, we heard that Will had been moved back to the ICU and was recovering from the anesthesia. He would be ready for a visit by his parents in a few minutes.

But the few minutes became a few hours as day turned into night. Unable to engage in small talk and stressed by the strained interactions of family, I took to walking the hall, where I overheard from some other hall-walkers that the cardiac ICU was currently closed due to an emergency procedure taking place, one that was sterile and required the involvement of most of the doctors and nurses on duty.

So those of us striding the halls passed each other in a grim, silent, elongated single-file circle, not looking in each other's eyes, and unsure if our hoping that our own beloved child was okay meant we were simultaneously wishing ill on our fellow travelers. Assuming, I think, that none of us knew which of the twelve children was in such bad shape, and knowing that asking would be the worst kind of cruelty.

My brain raced as I wondered if praying for my son meant praying for the misfortune of another child, or if my prayer should be more inclusive of all the patients behind those glass doors, and if that was even possible, both personally and theologically. Finally, I decided to quit thinking and praying and simply walk and allow myself to occasionally crane my neck to attempt to see where all the figures in gowns were gathered. I've trained for and run six marathons, but I can't recall a time when my legs felt heavier.

Eventually the chaos inside quieted to a degree, and a nurse from the medical team came out to speak to me and my wife, telling us that our son was stable, apologizing for not updating us, and inviting us to put on clean gowns so we could squeeze by the bed of the ailing child and see our own. Doing so seemed disrespectful, joined as we were to the other families still waiting outside. So we thanked the nurse for her consideration and let her go back inside. I rejoined the chain gang in the hallway, feeling a little guilty for my good news but committed to continue waiting in this slow-motion microcosm of the human race.

Several hours later, one of the families was invited into the "consultation room," which was the coded descriptor of the space where bad news was delivered. Good news is generally given bedside, but the disappointing stuff is doled out by committee to the family in some remote location. Usually the team of medical experts would crowd in, leaving just enough room for the essential family members. If the assembled staff was mostly white-coated doctors, one could be assured the news was not about death but of an ominous downturn in condition. On the other hand, death, or imminent death, meant the presence of a smaller group, more civilian and generally more female: chaplains and counselors that I associated with the Grim Reaper, along with a person in a blue security uniform who waited a few paces down the hall.

On this particular evening, it was a medical team, and after just a few minutes the door opened and a male figure exited, silently rushing down the hall to a destination unknown even to himself. In my observation, fathers usually bolted, while grandfathers and uncles stayed put. The interpretation seemed clear. It was bad news—bad but not final.

As this meeting continued, my wife and I were invited into the ICU to see our son, a huge relief and an unspeakable heartbreak, all at once. Still on a ventilator, he now had a large rack of monitors and meds parked next to his bed, and a whole array of big and small tubes going into and out of his body, along with thin wires that appeared from his abdomen, attached directly to his heart to enable the electrical pacing of its movements should it become necessary. He was recovered from the anesthesia, but was still on a paralytic drug that made his body limp, his eyes blank and open, staring into space. His chest was open to allow the swelling around the heart to decrease to the point that it could be safely closed. We could watch his heart beating behind a clear bandage. But the most alarming thing to me—or the only piece to which I could relate—was his temperature. I noted the number in centigrade, then waited for the opportunity to sneak a peek at the conversion chart posted on his bed, only to find it was far below any level recorded on his chart. It would be sometime the next day before I was able to register its slow, steady return to normal.

Exhausted and with nothing more to do, we updated our family, sent them to their hotels and hosts, and headed "home." Warned by the nurses of the strong possibility of a quick change in Will's condition, we had made arrangements to stay at a vacationing friend's house, located only three blocks away. So on that Friday night we walked through an inky alley in a heavy rain to the back door of the house. I fumbled with the key, then with the keypad of the alarm. It sounded in a deafening shrill as I reflexively ducked and started to run back out the door. I stopped, composed myself, caught my breath, felt for the light and tried the code again as I rehearsed what I would say to the police. When the alarm finally stopped echoing through the neighborhood, I carried in our luggage, shut the door, and leaned on the granite countertop to cry out my pent-up pain and stress and helplessness.

While I was doing this, my wife was trying to nurse our daughter, hoping against reason that her breast milk had started to flow. It was painful to see them pitted against each other: one of them screaming for milk, and the other stifling screams because she didn't have it to give, at least not yet. Finally, I swaddled all six pounds of Ella and tucked her into the stroller for a short night that would be interrupted by many more episodes of screaming. As always, we slept with both phones fully charged and set by the window for maximum cell signal in case we were summoned back to the hospital.

As promised, the milk did indeed "come in" two days later, on what will undoubtedly be the happiest Mother's Day of our lives. On Monday, Will's chest was closed and he started to receive tube feedings of fortified breast milk shortly thereafter. Ella's color turned less yellow as she took more milk.

That same week also brought a stroke for Will's great-grandfather and namesake. Several members of our family urgently drove all day to travel from our hospital to the hospital where he was languishing. Thankfully they made it, but only shortly before he passed away. Our attendance at the funeral was quite impossible, of course, but that didn't make our absence any less painful. As a kind of consolation I spent odd moments trying to write a eulogy to be delivered at his funeral. And in a kind of cosmic balance, some dear friends were married the following Saturday, and I was driven the several hours by other generous friends so I could deliver the wedding homily before hurrying back. The chance to join them was wonderful, but the shuttling between such disparate worlds gave me a kind of emotional whiplash.

The following Monday, still staying at our friends' place, I got up in the dark to drive to our home and drop off my wedding tuxedo and to gather my materials to teach the final session of an ethics course at a local university. After teaching the class, I hurried to pick up the girls and head to the hospital. In so doing I left my bag in the front seat, a split-second decision made in consideration of the broad daylight, busy street, and expectation of a brief stay inside.

I came out ten minutes later, burdened with many bags, a stroller, and a baby in a car seat carried behind me. I walked around the side of the car to see the street sparkling with shattered glass. So complete was my shock and my focus on the day ahead that my only thought was, *Well, okay, but we can still drive the car to the hospital for Ella's appointment with her pediatrician.* I tried to brainstorm methods of cleaning off the driver's seat and considered throwing down something to protect us from being cut on the brittle shards. The reality dawned slowly, as anyone who's suffered a robbery knows. First, I noticed the absence of our iPod, and felt sick. Then I noticed the bag was missing from the front seat.

The bag contained the final exams and final papers for the entire class I'd taught. The bag contained our laptop computer. *Oh, our new laptop. Oh no.* And it also held our digital camera. *Oh no, the photos of the kids.* But wait, we

had backed up those files! It would be okay! Moored in mo-
lasses, my brain slowly processed the awful truth: the files
were backed up . . . *on the computer*. And not having been
home more than fifteen minutes, we had not backed up the
laptop memory on our home hard drive. So the precious
photos were gone, gone, gone.

How could this be? On such a busy street, on such a bright
day, with all that we were dealing with? I walked up and
down the sidewalk, crying and pleading with anyone I could
find to help me determine who had taken my things so that
I could get them back. So I could pay any price, or take any
risk to have those photos back, those photos that might be
the last photos of our Will—photos irreplaceable and precious and impossibly missing. But no one knew anything, no
one had seen anything, no one could do anything. I prayed,
but somehow knew that God wouldn't do anything either.
God could have stopped this or changed this, I thought, but
didn't. So what was the point of asking God to miraculously
intercede after the fact? It was one of those days when one is
forced to concede that, yes, God and the universe *are* seemingly pitted against you.

The police officer who responded was calm and patient
to the point of being irritating. I wanted to run through the
streets in hopes that I could still spot someone, yet she was
obviously satisfied to complete a detailed report and head
back to the station. I slowed down and explained everything
and answered all her questions. No, I didn't have any enemies.
No, I didn't know who might do something like this. No, I
didn't have any girlfriends or affairs or secret admirers.

I took the opportunity to explain the dire condition of my
son, that the photos of his life were now missing, and that I
would do almost anything to get them back, even to the point
of trying to respond to the cryptic note left on the windshield
asking for some kind of meeting. Which the police officer

implored me to ignore, though she didn't seem inclined to follow up on it either. Mostly she told me to relax, repeatedly stating "everything is gonna be fine"—which I wanted to believe, but then realized she'd say this to anyone to calm them down since there was nothing anyone could do.

One year later, these are the details that lead one to another when I see the old box for that computer in the closet as we work at another session of spring-cleaning. Right next to the box are a whole bunch of other reminders. Will we ever be able to part with artifacts like Will's clothes, medical files, and a box full of cards of congratulations at his birth mixed with cards of condolences?

What about the blankets that swaddled him once we brought him home—do we really need to keep them all or are there just a few that are special?

Or should we keep all of it right here and try to have another child?

Is it too soon to think about such things?

When will we be able to begin again or stop this endless rehashing?

Do I need counseling?

Will I ever be done with all of this?

More to the point, will I ever want to move on?

My Confession

Some of my deepest shame around the things we did and didn't do in the midst of our rawest grief surfaced one day when we greedily indulged ourselves at a nearby outlet mall.

It happened in the days following the funeral as our hectic life slowly ebbed back to what suddenly seemed to be an unnaturally slow pace and an unnerving kind of quiet. The final step came when we drove the last guest to the airport, said good-bye at the security line, and aimlessly strolled back to the car. The baby was ready for a nap in her car seat and my wife and I were settling into our spots when one of us made the pregnant observation, "Well, we're halfway to the outlet mall." The suggestion was clear, as was the recognition that the alternative of going home and staring at the walls until bedtime was simply unbearable.

Without saying so, we knew what was at stake. We would waste a significant amount of money in exchange for a few hours of freedom from our troubles and some trinkets. So we drove to the mall, ate fried food at the food court, and chased it down with fancy coffee drinks. We rented a stroller to carry our girl and our indulgences, and struck out through the sunny mall that was meant to look like some impossibly elongated small town square.

Looking back, I realize it was more than just an escape (if you ever get the chance, walk into a store and answer the ubiquitous question, "Can I help you find anything?" with the response, "Oh, it doesn't much matter what we buy; we're here for retail therapy!" and see what happens). No, it was more than just that—it was our finding our most blissful comfort zone. Trained by our culture to strive, acquire, and spend, we embraced the false identity of *consumer*. Here, we were in charge, powerful, determining our own fate, appearance, and future. Here, we could move ourselves, and no one could stop us.

And move we did. From store to store we'd pick up the car seat in which our baby was nestled, shove our newly acquired treasures into the dark recesses of the stroller, and just keep on shopping. Like a drunk without a hangover, we were intentionally unaware and unaffected by the mounting pile of merchandise. Just about the time our guilt intruded in earnest, the caffeine jolt from the overpriced coffee kicked in and we floated above our better judgment. It was euphoric.

The results were predictable. We lavished our daughter with hip new clothes and cute shoes, and treated my wife to some stylish dresses to match her shrinking shape, as well as trendy jeans and fresh tops. I bought at least three black shirts, and momentarily considered new running clothes now that the opportunity to leave the house seemed possible. But mostly I bought things that would make me feel good and fresh and young and yet show the world a slice of the darkness within. At one store I hit pay dirt, a kind of hyphenated trifecta: some eco-friendly, fair-trade, rock-star jeans and a complementary blazer to match, all marked down to below fifty percent. This was perfect. I could assuage my general and particular guilt with the knowledge I was enriching and empowering some good people in Tanzania. Deal done!

We returned to the same store nine months later. I felt embarrassed by my previous foolishness, even as the spirit of this modern temple offered forgiveness for my sins and promised redemption through further indulgence. I looked around the racks to tempt fate, less desperate this time, more reflective and more wary. And yet I still felt compelled to buy another black T-shirt. This one featured the stylized form of an elongated cross and a sword in the shape of an X, all overlaid with a skull. Underneath, the inscription read *Death Is Not the End*. A campy sentiment that I would have had a hard time affirming nine months ago, but which I found myself reaching for now, even though it was $29.99. Less than 15 percent off.

Ghosts

I'm sick of this mess in my head. Ordinary details of my life jump off the page and hit me on the chin, throwing me off-balance and making me stumble. How can I heal when so many details conspire against me? The sense of hopefulness growing within me is tenuous, indeed.

I'm away on a family vacation, reading a novel whose main character is named Will, who has a "disfigured" face and a life-threatening heart condition that is progressing as he nears thirty. I don't even notice these details at first, but suddenly I connect the dots and feel empty, betrayed. Why can't I just read this book without feeling so encumbered? I'm on vacation, after all, sitting by the pool, and the author is clearly using the name Will as a literary device, and so too the disfiguration and heart condition. He's making a statement, not writing about me or my little boy, yet I have a hard time picking up the book again.

Caught in this angst, I look to my right, where my daughter sleeps. In an instant I flash back to three years ago, when I sat in a similar chair at a similar resort in a similar tourist town in Mexico, when I read a thick work of nonfiction about genetic engineering and the ethics of biotechnology. A book that passed for relaxed reading as I tried to make the weighty decision of whether we should attempt in vitro fertilization and face all the ethical, practical, and financial implications of such a decision. Now I have a little girl sleeping on a beach towel next to me, and I have the memory of her brother. In this moment I understand that she is an anchor; she keeps me from being dashed on the rocks, and she keeps me from going anywhere too fast. For better and for worse, she keeps me from running away from my life, and so I simultaneously revere her and resent her in this moment.

This same morning I had been walking around the posh resort as workers scuttled and swept and pruned and did all the things that make it look completely natural, only better. As I ambled around trying to get my daughter to sleep in my arms, I noticed that one of the more solitary gardeners had an obviously repaired cleft lip. I noticed and confirmed this quickly in the two seconds it takes to smile and nod at someone. In the next second I realized we probably didn't share a language, and anyway I wouldn't have anything profitable to say to him. I wasn't staring, but I would if it weren't rude. Because I wanted to look into his eyes to try to understand what hardships he had faced in school and life, and to let him know that I empathized in some small way. And that although there wasn't any demonstrable way for me to show I understood, I felt a little of his pain and alienation anyway.

Months before, I was at the supermarket, waiting at the meat counter with my daughter in the cart in front of me. I've found that many of the people shopping at 8 a.m. are parents with their young kids, trying to avoid traffic and maximize the productive periods of the day between naps. With our commonalities (and sleep deprivation) we tend to be talkative and inquisitive, asking about ages and developmental milestones and trading food tips. Today was no exception. A mom with a talkative toddler at her side and a rotund infant in the cart complimented my daughter and asked all of the requisite questions. I returned the favor and heard my brain grind to a halt when she mentioned her son's name, and felt the world twist as I choked back tears, then finally walked away thankful that the adult participants in such conversations only look at the kids.

Another day found me walking through one of those big-box stores near our house. My eye passed over an unremarkable toy: a plastic turtle with a miniature aquarium built into his back. Unremarkable but for the fact it was the same toy gifted to our boy shortly after his birth, and had endlessly entertained him in his bed, and has sat at the back of our deepest closet for nine months now. I turned away from this too, for I didn't want to cast a shadow over an otherwise pleasant shopping trip with my wife and daughter.

When given a choice, I find myself preferring to occasionally administer the tiny doses of medicine to our daughter via eyedropper-type tubes rather than the more precise oral syringes. After many hundreds of repetitions, I am unconsciously expert at using one hand to draw up the meds, to push any air pockets to the top of the syringe, and to carefully remove any excess medicine until the dosage is precisely correct. But doing so reminds me of my boy, and of our unreasonable faith that these elixirs would prolong his life. So I use the eyedropper instead.

On the way back from our vacation, our daughter was sleeping on her mother's lap, lying on one of those white pillows provided by the airline. And without any realization of why we might be doing it, my wife and I both began to worry about her breathing, fretting and checking her pulse and exchanging worried glances before we each wordlessly realized we were both being unconsciously reminded of the pillow that held Will's head inside his casket. "I don't like her to lie on white pillows, ever," one of us confessed, to the instant agreement of the other. So we did our best to slow our own breathing, trying to calm ourselves while resigning to the fact that, at 38,000 feet, we would only be able to say good-bye anyway. Again.

At the hospital where she works, my wife recognized one of our son's surgeons visiting from his hospital across town. Halting yet somehow compelled, my wife approached and introduced herself, reminding him that he had operated on our son. The surgeon kindly inquired as to his name.

When I heard that the surgeon recognized the name, and that he was "a little guy" and that he was strong, I burst forth with sobs of both joy and grief. After I composed myself, my wife related that when the surgeon asked, "How is he doing?" and she answered that our son had died, he caught himself and remembered this fact, though we'd never expect him to. But somehow, to know that Will's life and spirit were remembered, and that he was respected, was deeply moving.

Leaning over the counter in our kitchen, I went from happy to wailing in two seconds flat, deep sobs pouring forth. But my grimace must have looked like a grin, for my daughter grabbed on to my leg, smiled at me, and laughed a bright and hearty laugh. So I picked her up and held her close, my painful tears pushed up against her beautiful smile and illustrating perfectly the tension I felt. Sad and happy, pained and delighted, shackled by the past and yet somehow hopeful about the future.

Sharing Burdens

I don't usually talk to people on planes. Air travel, in my humble opinion, is a time and place for reading. When we were first married and my slightly nervous wife wanted me to hold her hand during the takeoff and landing, I would generally do so, but would intermittently retract the hand to turn pages. So when I'm on a plane, I usually indulge myself in the normally antisocial practice of reading in the middle of a crowd of people.

But since I've started traveling with our daughter, we have a relational bridge to those seated around us. Sometimes the bridge is burning, as when we were once taxiing before takeoff and Ella started crying and fussing. "Not for two hours!"

harrumphed the man in front of us, mature in years but only slightly more patient than our one-year-old.

Most of the time we've noticed that people tend to withhold conversational connection until the flight has ended, or at least until it is headed toward a happy conclusion. If our girl has been quiet, they will smile and say how pretty and well behaved she is (if she's been a bit noisy, they just force a smile, eyebrows raised). On one flight, the lady sitting next to me followed this formula, turning toward us just after the pilot proudly informed us that we were beginning our final descent and we all moved our seats to their forward position and our tray tables to their upright position and we securely stowed any baggage. Our new friend mentioned that her travels to Mexico would involve reuniting with a friend whose husband had died twenty-nine years earlier, and noted that she herself had lost her husband recently, and that she was just starting to get out and socialize. Thinking that she might want to say more, I pushed my luck and asked how long her husband had been gone. Stiffening slightly, she offered a sidelong glance and an atonal "Three months."

Feeling her discomfort, I offered my condolences and explained that we had twins and that we had lost our Will just eight months earlier.

"Oh," she said matter-of-factly, appearing relieved now. "Then you know."

Which illustrated to me the tension in which all of us exist: All of us have suffered, or will suffer, loss. This fact firmly in place, the idealist in me asserts that all of us should be able to empathize. If we haven't gone through exactly what our neighbor has, we can surely extrapolate what we do know, and have experienced, and at least come alongside them. We should be able to connect with anyone, and everyone.

But at the same time, no one knows like those who've lost, and especially those who have suffered a recent loss. Widows will gather for silent understanding, orphaned children will connect with others, and parents with suddenly empty cribs will unite in solidarity, however silent. We attended a grief group on a Saturday at the hospital, and before we had even spoken to one another, a kind of comfortable—if gloomy— camaraderie was immediately present with those who had gathered.

I shouldn't try to build a system here, I know. It wouldn't be fair to ask those who are grieving to suspend the process of their grief indefinitely so they can help others for whom grief is fresh. It wouldn't be fair to task everyone with the hard work of helping someone else when it is all they can do to, in the words of one supportive friend, "just put your pants on every day." And it's not fair to carry forward the assumption that true empathy is impossible: that only those who have felt the exact experience can help others do the same. Yet it is good and helpful to give a hand and share the burden of someone else—to join in the universal conversation of love and loss. In so doing, we might be reaching forward through time, anticipating our feelings of loss and grief when our dear ones depart. Or we might be reaching back through time, dredging up feelings of abandonment and anger that we'd rather forget. In any case, our words should be few. But facing this fundamental part of being human is essential.

Exhaustion

Summer

A couple of days ago, on the third day of summer, I was talking to the man who farms an organic plot that produces an amazing variety of vegetables for us and a few friends, and we were, predictably, talking about plants and weather. Specifically, when we could expect the tomatoes to ripen to their delectable peak of ripeness and delight us with dirt-tinged bites straight from the vine. Like any good botanist or retailer, he was comparing this year to last season, and noting the obvious differences in the weather. Whether he said that last season was rainier or drier, I cannot say, for the simple mention of the weather last summer kicked my brain into a scary tailspin.

I cannot remember what the weather was like last summer.

Growing up in a farm family, and being a dedicated fisherman during my childhood and teen years, and going for a run nearly every day for several years, I am generally very attuned to the weather. But last year I existed in a kind of hermetic and antiseptic existence, shuttling myself in a sealed silver container between home and hospital, hospital and home, day after day after day. The completely nondescript days all blended together and I started to wear a watch so that I could

151

tell what day it was and avoid the embarrassment of walking into a cafeteria when it had just closed early on Sunday, or being trapped by Friday gridlock, or letting on that I didn't know it was Memorial Day or the Fourth of July or whatever.

In my world, the weather was just something that followed me as I ran from car to building laden with baby and bags and worries barely slowing me down. *Weather* didn't register as I clicked the baby into her car seat and placed each bag in its assigned place in the car trunk. Mine was a climate-controlled existence, bland beyond description, distinctive only by the particular travail my son was facing on any given day.

On most days that summer, the main travail was his breathing. As a still-tiny patient who was recovering from serious heart surgery and trying to adjust to a compromised circulatory system and a large cleft in the roof of his mouth, his breathing was done by a mechanical ventilator. At first, the hospital staff was happy enough that he was alive and recovering and relatively stable. But after a few days, the goal was set: Will needed to come off the vent. The first step was abrupt and hopeful. The tube was removed, he was given a breathing treatment to reduce the swelling in his throat, and everyone took their place to observe his progress. I walked into the CICU that morning to see him free of the breathing equipment, panting away. Incredulous, I cheered him on before rushing out to the waiting room to change places with Stacy, who was watching our daughter. But by the time she hurried back, he'd already gone into respiratory distress and had to be re-intubated.

Subsequent attempts were both carefully planned and random. One day, a nurse was checking on an alarm on the ventilator and saw the source of the problem. Our little ruffian had reached into his mouth to pull the tube from his throat. Rather than immediately reinserting the tube, the team gathered to observe him for several hours. He continued to breathe on his own before he was again intubated. The tape holding the tube was more securely fastened, along with a more careful swaddling of his hands.

But most of the time, his ventilator settings would be tweaked to deliver less air pressure, and to do so less frequently, allowing his lungs and muscles to do some work on their own while still giving him a safety net. After a few of these successful "trials," the ventilator would be removed and he would be on his own again. He would lie there, somewhere between awake and asleep, panting away in the most labored way. At those times I would be filled with a mixture of pride and pity and gripped in a kind of involuntary, empathetic, substitutionary effort.

When he failed the trial, we all caught our breath, and he would be allowed to rest for several days to regain strength and weight in the hope that he'd be able to overcome this challenge later. So we were obsessed with his weight and his breathing, caught on the horns of the dilemma whereby breathing cost him energy and therefore weight, and yet additional weight provided strength for breathing. We watched the ventilator and held our breath as his tube feedings were incrementally increased in both volume and caloric concentration. It was a thick, palpable tension that we felt.

Summer also brought our friends—beautiful, dedicated people who brought us meals every day and cared for us and shopped for us and delivered hope and hugs. And yet it seemed our helplessness was contagious, and our stresses put cracks in their psyche, allowing advice to leak out. This was a source of searing pain, more obviously evident than the actual physical pain right in front of me. It was handy and easy to displace this pain, of course, but that is not to suggest the alienation I felt as they prattled on—about how we should take a day off, or get our son on a different feeding regimen, or about their tough day at work—was not real, too. I tried my best to appreciate their sacrifice, to cultivate grace and gratefulness, but I remember with shame multiple occasions when I'd finish the food they had brought and instantly pray that they would leave right then, and leave me to my tiny, crowded world. There was no room for them inside of me.

On some days—sometimes by effort, sometimes by accident—I found that I was able to connect. It helped me even to focus on the pains and challenges and joys of their lives. Other days were triage days, and I was indignant and offended that they even had difficulties, much less a willingness to share them with me. And I was bothered that their lives were infringing on mine. Even though they brought me meals—preservative-free, mostly purchased from the high-end grocery store ready-made kitchens at no small expense—delivered via claustrophobic suburban and city traffic with love and deep concern for our physical and mental health, and even though they were praying and rooting for us, and even though I knew my life was a much greater infringement on theirs, I didn't have the capacity to be a good friend to them. It was not until many months later that my failing them even registered on the emotional spreadsheet inside my heart, and months afterward that their perceived offenses began to be worn down by time and grace.

This magnification of personal offenses, both perceived and real, suffered at the hands of both God and people, is frightening, even when it's happening. Even in the midst of the emotional turmoil of feeling betrayed, I could see I was teetering on a sharp point between selfishness and self-preservation. I could see myself engaging in this insular introspection and I hoped I could wean myself from these occasional indulgences for the sake of my friends and family, and for the sake of God and myself.

May and June rushed by, each day blending into the next, until those many days became seemingly one long day. This two-month day was spent in ICUs, for the most part. We were there every hour we were possibly available, even though there was precious little for us to do but stand by Will's side and watch him fight to breathe, and to watch the charts for hopeful signs of weight gain.

By the end of June he finally found the strength to turn the corner on his breathing. He was breathing so well, in fact, we were left wondering what all the fuss was about. On his last day in the ICU, a team of physical therapists and speech therapists came by to feed him by mouth and to train us in the same. This was absolutely terrifying, but also affirming and engaging—we at least had something to do now, some contribution to his care, some tangible task with which to engage. We would feed him every three hours that he was awake, with much of the downtime taken up by prep and cleanup.

Shortly after he was released from the ICU to a more conventional department in the heart and kidney unit, he was transferred to a subacute care facility a few miles away. I was terrified of this too—that we were being shuffled away to languish, that the subacute care would be substandard, that we'd never check out of this place that was sometimes called "long-term care"—but I tried my best to put on a brave face and accept the inevitable. I rode in the ambulance for the transport, air-conditioning blasting on a hot day, country music playing on the radio, strained small talk with the driver, with me clutching the backpack I carried every day like some kind of totem of familiarity.

When Will's bed was parked in his new spot along the wall, and his oxygen and sensors were all set up, I tried to engage with the staff psychologist there, to answer her questions and perform small talk in a psychologically sophisticated way, but I was too tired to think. When the speech therapist came by, I tried to subtly let her know what I had learned at the hospital, without acting as though my prior training would eclipse the training she would give me. I was learning to let each person I met lead me, and to allow their expertise to take temporary precedence before I invoked other, earlier training.

So in a sense, I missed the summer. The days and nights and weeks all ran together, blurred in a rush of full-time caretaking. We rarely stepped outside to see or feel the sun, and stayed insulated in our cool cocoon of air-conditioning. But in another sense, Will was our summer, shining his light on our lives.

Belief/Unbelief

When they came to the other disciples, they saw a large crowd around them and the teachers of the law arguing with them. As soon as all the people saw Jesus, they were overwhelmed with wonder and ran to greet him.

"What are you arguing with them about?" he asked.

A man in the crowd answered, "Teacher, I brought you my son, who is possessed by a spirit that has robbed him of speech. Whenever it seizes him, it throws him to the ground. He foams at the mouth, gnashes his teeth and becomes rigid. I asked your disciples to drive out the spirit, but they could not."

"You unbelieving generation," Jesus replied, "how long shall I stay with you? How long shall I put up with you? Bring the boy to me."

So they brought him. When the spirit saw Jesus, it immediately threw the boy into a convulsion. He fell to the ground and rolled around, foaming at the mouth.

Jesus asked the boy's father, "How long has he been like this?"

"From childhood," he answered. "It has often thrown him into fire or water to kill him. But if you can do anything, take pity on us and help us."

"'If you can'?" said Jesus. "Everything is possible for one who believes."

Immediately the boy's father exclaimed, "I do believe; help
me overcome my unbelief!"

Mark 9:14–24

I don't ask questions and make complaints of God because
I fail to believe, but because I do believe. I believe that God
exists, and that I'll find peace and some way to go on with my
life. I believe that God and God's kingdom are permeating
this planet, remaking the world into the place where things are
done "on earth as they are in heaven." It is because of these
beliefs that I see my own unbelief. I see the pieces that do not
seem to fit into that picture. Some things stand out, stick out,
refuse to yield to my reasoning or emotional opposition. Like
a cowlick on a kid's head, they refuse to lie down, no matter
how persistently I comb them. And I don't want to ignore
them or pretend they're not there. I don't want to plaster the
cowlick or push the discordant pieces into the background.

My wife and I love each other very much. We value our
relationship, enough to fight over it. And we do. We don't
generally argue about issues, but we do argue about engagement and communication (we went to college together, and
took some of the same psychology classes). If we notice a
terse tone or a raised voice, we'll call it out, and frequently
have an argument over it. But we always say that we love each
other. This can seem strange when we're pitched in heated
debate, arguing about what the other said or did. But it makes
sense to us—it is this very love that we're fighting about, that
we're fighting for.

I love God. I love God enough to argue, to protest and
debate, and to get sad and angry. Like Jacob, I'm ready to
wrestle with God, even if it means I'll get hurt. Like the na-
tion that Jacob fathered, I'd be honored to be called *Israel*,
which means "one who struggles with God." I'd rather walk
with a limp than just cruise through life on the handed-down

faith and answers of someone else. To, hopefully, find myself and my God at the end of all of this. Not that I'll get all my questions answered—I'd be disappointed to find that there is some simple explanation to all my pain, to be honest—but that I'll find some satisfying middle ground, some passable peace, some relatively stable ground to walk on as I continue my journey through the rest of my life.

I want to take everything—my belief and my doubts—and lay all of it on the table. I want to be honest with others, but more important, to be honest with myself. Because I'm looking for much more than just mental assent. I want to live out all of my beliefs, and all of my doubts. I want to live in the tension between faith and doubt. I want to live in the real world, with all its joys and heartbreaks. Which is why stifling my feelings toward God seems dangerous, and disingenuous.

Sometimes, when I'm arguing with my wife about a miscommunication, I'll mention a perception that will strike her as quite damning. I'll say she seemed insincere, or unkind, or harsh when I well know she is wholeheartedly kind and gentle. Occasionally she'll take offense and say something like, "How could you think that? Don't you trust me?" and I'll struggle for words and try to avoid digging a deeper hole than I'm already in: "Of course I trust you—that's why I feel the need to share these perceptions that just don't fit what I know about you!" This is hard for me to say, and harder still for her to hear. But if our relationship is valuable, then it deserves this kind of time and attention, honesty and deconstruction. If it is solid, it will withstand our use of it and our abuse of it, our efforts to strip away the decorative facades and misunderstandings.

In losing my son, I don't think that God has enacted or allowed some evil to be done to me. Quite the contrary, I'm more aware than ever of my own freedom of will, of my own responsibility and ability to act in God's interests, and of my failure to do so with integrity. And I'm not interested in parsing out the difference between God's culpability and my responsibility. My feelings are much more base than that: I just think God seems a little unkind just now. Harsh. Unfeeling. Indifferent. Unconcerned. And yet deeper and more profoundly, I have a confidence in God's goodness, mercy, compassion, and interest in me. I'm trying to reconcile these things.

I trust God, so I question God. I love God, yet I doubt God. I believe, and so I ask for help in my unbelief.

Letting Go

As July passes by, I find myself reliving the events of last summer in ways I haven't before, even when I was actually living the events. A year ago, life came at such a breakneck pace that I currently find myself in a kind of posttraumatic stress recapitulation of the events, my mind organizing the narrative and trying to bring order to all the feelings I was experiencing.

Almost a year ago we were leaving the children's hospital. Stabilized after surgery and finally getting off the ventilator, Will needed to gain weight and the doctors were hoping to wean him off his supplemental oxygen, so they discharged us to a subacute care facility several miles away. From my current perspective I understand this change in venue was innocuous, if not helpful and hopeful. But then, I remember feeling out of control, displaced, disrespected, and angry as I followed my five-pound son, who was cartoonishly dwarfed by the full-sized stretcher being loaded into the ambulance.

Even at the time I knew that much of my worry was in my imagination, rooted in my own fatigue and fear, related to a general anxiety of going from what was known to what was unknown, and this feeling being exacerbated by my low-level exhaustion. Once our family settled into the rhythms of life at this facility, the stakes were raised by the fact that there was so little for me to do. Besides resting, Will ate every three hours, so there was about one hour of intense work of prepping his bottle and feeding him, followed by two hours of waiting. That's too much time to think, too much time to wonder what you might do differently, and entirely too much time to imagine how the staff might distrust and disrespect you and your efforts.

One nurse in particular was a wonderful, friendly and generous woman, even in my own darkened memory. At the time, however, I was sure she was trying to undermine my efforts through some combination of anti-male discrimination, control issues, and general lack of concern for my son and our family. In fact, the reason she was reluctant to give me much of the breast milk out of the refrigerator was no doubt due to the fact it was precious, and Will didn't drink much of it by bottle. But to me it was important to bring a sizable bottle to the meal as a sign of my hope and confidence in a fruitful feed, and in case this meal was the one that he would finally finish. Yet in her conservative ways she hesitated to pour out much milk for me or to respond to my kind requests for a tiny bit more milk.

I became obsessed with this tension, replaying interactions in my mind, analyzing them, committing to sit with Will every single minute I was there—whether he was awake or asleep—and only leaving with an important and clearly stated purpose, along with an offer to bring back anything she might want: a snack, a meal, a donut, a cup of coffee. The fact that she politely declined these offers seemed to be mean and unkind, intended to frustrate me. Looking back, I'm certain she was supportive and had only the best of intentions.

Before we moved from the hospital, I had another nemesis (whether imaginary or real, I'm still unsure). She was a bright and chipper nurse practitioner, who welcomed us to a new room on a new floor and explained that we were there to get Will stronger and for us to get training so that we could take him home as soon as possible. The very next day I was listening to the doctors and nurses who visited the room for rounds, and she casually mentioned moving my boy to a "long-term care facility," which made my blood run cold and my face glow hot, simultaneously. Our social worker saw my alarm and lingered for a few minutes to empathize and reframe the forced move as a helpful transfer. "Subacute care facility" is the way she described it, and the different terminology was immediately empowering and hopeful.

A couple of days later, one of our doctors brought up a tiny concern about a specific dose of a particular medicine, thwarting the general plan to expedite the transfer for that day. Even in the moment I suspected she was simply giving me one more day of some sense of control, one more day to accept this huge decision that was completely out of my hands. And even as I write this, the love and care communicated by that gesture couched in minutiae and medicine brings tears to my eyes. I am quite sure that if I ever mentioned it to her, she would deny any ulterior motive (and she'd probably be right).

The challenge of being so impaired while under such scrutiny was palpable, and constant. From the moment we arrived at Will's bedside in the morning to the time we drove home at night, to every late night and early morning phone call of inquiry, we were driven by the desire to be perceived as the perfect parents and caregivers. Throughout every single day we were painstakingly polite to each other, and to every single person on the staff. When a nurse misunderstood the doctor's order that only parents and occupational therapists feed our son by mouth, and instead gave him a bottle one morning before we arrived, we were outraged and infuriated by what seemed like an obvious conspiracy, but we spoke in low tones and with gentle questions.

When one of the overly helpful laundry workers overlooked a posted sign and took one of Will's favorite shirts and it was never returned, we were heartbroken, but made only the meekest of inquiries as to its return, since we didn't want to show our obvious desperation and imbalance over the whole affair.

When the social workers offered us a chance to stay in a specially designed apartment to practice giving Will 24-hour care, we dug into the windowless room with a fierce resolve to prove ourselves as caring and competent, as independent and teachable, and to do so for every day that the room was available.

After almost a week, we started to realize with shock and horror that we were perceived as overstaying our welcome, of taking advantage of their hospitality, and we agonized over how to rectify the situation and salvage our reputations. The weight of our responsibilities, multiplied by the sheer number of relational connections—doctors, nurses, administrators, custodial staff, cafeteria workers, social workers, medical liaisons—was almost unbearable, and ultimately unmanageable.

I suppose in the end we proved ourselves, and we're eternally grateful for the training and the adept changes in venues for care (for him) and training (for us) that allowed us to bring him home despite the continued presence of both oxygen and a nasogastric feeding tube. And I realize that, one year later, I still need to let go of this desire to control outcomes and manage perceptions, if not for the sake of these wonderful and well-intentioned people, then for my own mental health. It's just that, one year later, I can't shake the thought that if I'd been more aware of certain details of his life, more attuned to the particular challenges he faced, and more engaged with his care, he'd still be with us. I want to change what cannot be changed.

Lifting My Eyes

Overcoming Memory

The great marathoner Bill Rodgers is famous for saying that you can't begin training for your next marathon until you've forgotten how much your last marathon hurt. As we consider the two months between our "today" and the one-year anniversary of Will's death, we cannot help but think about what we'll do next. Strictly speaking we declared this first year off-limits for moving, quitting jobs, planning for the future, or making any real decisions. "We'll talk about all of that after September," is the promise we make to ourselves, meant to give us room to grieve and to free us from our sometimes obsessive worrying about what will come.

Of course, rules like this are made to be broken, and we do occasionally indulge in forward-thinking. Most especially, about the rest of our family. You see, when we did our first round of IVF, there were four zygotes that developed to the point of being viable. The decision of how many to transfer was a huge one: big enough to make me wonder once again if people should even be making these kinds of decisions. I worried that we had in fact crossed some line of the natural order when we took matters—namely, eggs and sperm—into our figurative hands.

"Two" was what we decided, and we were both joyful and fearful when we learned that, in spite of the odds, both of them had successfully implanted. The other two were put into a cryogenic freezer: "our two kidsickles" is how we've referred to them ever since.

We worried about them when we were concerned that Will's challenges were genetic, and we rejoiced for them when we learned his challenges were developmental only. But now we know the odds for a recurrence of similar problems are twice as high for subsequent siblings.

I worry and think about this quite a lot, in spite of my pledges to the contrary. And I wonder how and when we should transfer these two embryos, and if we should do them one at a time or double down as before. But I don't think about not transferring them. These are our kids, as far as I'm concerned. I'm not sure what I think about all this, so I keep the particulars at arms' length, knowing we'll do something after this fall.

But the other day I was eavesdropping on a phone conversation between my wife and her mother. They were talking about our "kids in the freezer," and somehow the psychic space I felt from these issues and concerns and questions suddenly gave me some clarity and perspective. Of course I want to try to have these kids, the sooner the better. I love them and deeply desire to know them and care for them. And I'll do so, even if that means another round of biweekly prenatal ultrasounds, and another child in the CICU, and another season of life crowded to overflowing with feedings and hospital visits. I'm not as naive as I used to be; I now know just how much that will cost in terms of money and energy and time and sanity. I now know what an unbearable strain it will put on the relationships of family and friends. But I surprised myself by recognizing that this is a small price to pay for another person, especially my own flesh and blood.

Shift

The light must be different in my coffee shop today, because when I looked at the tall barista with the short hair, he didn't look like the doctor who ran Will's code, not at all. And when he stepped away from his station to pour me my cup of plain coffee, he didn't sound like him at all either. It seems that my brain and my emotions are loosening their grip on the past and sparing me the constant re-envisioning and re-remembering of that awful night. I recognize this with some regret, as I am still worried that *letting go* will result in *forgetting*, that the memories will tarnish if I don't keep polishing them.

The further I go in this process of walking on, the more I think about the first steps. I'm less disappointed about Will's difficult life, less begrudging of his death, which is starting to seem merciful, and more stuck on first causes. I'm asking fewer questions about particular *why*s, and more questions about the general *why*:

Why did he need to have these anomalies in the first place? How and when did they occur?

Can I do research to determine the probable time frame for the onset of these developmental defects, and then correlate that to last fall's calendar?

What were we doing on the day his problems began?

What environmental factors were present that week?

What did we eat?

Did we do something differently, or should we have done something differently?

All of which takes me on a circuitous route to the bigger question: Why did this happen to us?

You don't ask questions like these in the midst of such trials. You imagine that your family and friends are asking them, and so you rely on them to cover these bases. You think that you should ask these kinds of questions, and you entertain the thought for a minute, but they're too complicated to shift and sort, and the results would be unproductive at best. If you blame yourself now, you will stall out at a time when *action* is called for. If you blame someone else, or some other physiological function, you will be equally stymied. But mostly you don't entertain these questions because they don't matter. Or maybe they *do* matter, but in the rush of the eternal moment that stretches before you, filled as it is with endless questions and decisions and execution of said decisions, they *can't* matter.

When you're doing triage with your children, your life, your relationships, your jobs, and your mental health, you are overloaded. You're too busy dealing with the reality right before you—this needy child and his twin sister and all it will take to bring them into the world. And if you believe in God, you feel as though you must table these overwhelming questions and declare an emergency non-escalation clause with your Maker and ask for help in going forward. You move because you must, marshalling every resource at your disposal to do so, and casting everything else to the side.

But with the curse and blessing of time—time to think, time to reflect, time to grieve, time to let go of some things and pick others up—the queries come back around to those base questions. Though it seems like an embarrassing cliché, I find that I cannot help but ask the question "Why me?" Why us? Why our family? I perform a cursory scan of my life, reviewing the episodes of challenge and disappointment and failure, and feel as though I'm being picked on, persecuted, singled out. In my impetuousness, I want to let myself say, Why me? Haven't we been through enough? So when some friends confide their prayers and misgivings to this effect (though I always dutifully respond by balancing the admitted difficulties of our life with the blessings) I secretly feel vindicated that they pester God with these questions.

I want Will back, of course. But I want him whole. I want his essence, the strong-spirited boy who would become a man without encumbrance or undue trial or suffering. I want to rewind to the day or days when his midline—his heart and mouth and umbilical cord—were formed, and I want to re-work the plumbing and push together the facial features so he can be free from limitation and a lifetime of second glances. I want him to be a regular kid.

The day before yesterday was a perfect summer Sunday afternoon. Bright skies, a steady breeze, and a non-humidified eighty-three degrees. The perfect day for my wife to take a nap before her weekly night shift in labor and delivery, and for Ella and me to follow up her own afternoon nap with a stroll to the park and the toddler-sized playground that sits in the dappled shade of tall trees. It was also the auspicious occasion of Ella's first unaided walk all the way from the car to our apartment, including each of the stone and wooden steps along the way. As well, it had also been the occasion of her first unassisted climb up the playground equipment (wide-eyed and grinning all the way), and first solo utterance of "Duh, dah, deee!" (a.k.a., "One, two, three!") and self-propulsion down the slide, squealing the whole way. And it was the first time she rode in the swing as something more than a sack of potatoes, methodically leaning backward and forward to aid in the effort.

I was ecstatically happy about all of this, but I was also shot through with sadness, involuntary tears distorting my view of these milestones. Much as I tried to avoid the feeling, I missed Will, wanted him to be here, wanted to celebrate *his* achievements and *his* joy at life.

In my imagination and idealism and wrestling with God, I'm no longer willing to accept these limitations—I want Will whole, racing his sister up the steps, jostling for position at the top of the slide, flashing rudimentary sign language cues, speaking nascent English, and inventing a special language with his twin sister whereby they can entertain and amuse each other, their shoulders shaking with laughter like their great-grandfather, and grandfather, and father.

I want it all. This may be an unreasonable demand, a stage of grief, a temporary station along the path. But it feels more right and more hopeful to long for a whole boy, rather than one who clung to life every day, his skin blue with the labored effort of insufficient oxygenation, his cleft lip and palate making it that much harder to eat and breathe and grow and thrive. I'd take him back in any condition, of course. I'd carry him through any obstacle, struggle with him through every encumbrance, trade my comfort for his pain at any hour of the day or night. But if I'm going to dream, I want to dream about wholeness. If I'm going to question God, I want to ask the hardest questions, to ask God the first questions. If I'm going to love my son, I want to remember his very essence, and not his compromised condition.

Monkey

This past weekend we attended a birthday party where our superhuman friend and all-around über-parent put together an incredible homegrown theme party around a popular children's television show. As she collaborated with her five-year-old son to design it, they realized they should recruit some help—namely, a couple of men to play the part of two mischievous spider monkeys. And apparently, for some reason I was afraid to ask, my name was immediately put at the top of the list. I tried to take the nomination in stride, doing my best to research the role sufficiently so that I might better get into character, and limbering up so that I could run around while dragging my knuckles through the grass.

My fellow monkey was one of the birthday boy's uncles, an acquaintance I see several times a year when we catch up at birthday parties, the occasional social event, or church service project. He is a great guy, of generous spirit and firm handshake. So when I greeted him, I wondered why I felt such strong and negative emotions toward him. I felt a knot in my throat, a tightness in my gut, a hitch in my shoulders, and I puzzled about the source of my negativity.

The answer wasn't long in coming. Very quickly I remembered that he had come to the funeral, and though that roomful of faces was a blur, I later heard that he hadn't actually attended the service itself but avoided it by intentionally busying himself with organizational details. At the time, I was more than hurt—I was indignant, and not only because I wanted him to hear my eulogy. I understood there must have been some very important reason why he didn't feel comfortable attending funerals—this one, another one, or any one—and yet I simply didn't care. In my head I assembled an argument that facing death and grief is simply part of being human, a line of reasoning that allowed no cop-out of any kind. He was a bad and selfish person in my mind, period. End of story.

But now I looked at him (before he put on the monkey mask) and realized I hardly knew him, really. He is only indirectly connected to me—the brother-in-law of my good friend—but he and his wife had taken time off from their important jobs to spend most of the day in a hot church building, preparing for and cleaning up after the funeral of a person they had never met. Yet in spite of that, I had overlooked his sacrifice and service and had insolently demanded even more. Worse, I hadn't even tried to understand why he was hesitant to attend the service—what tragic loss he had suffered, or what fear shackled him—nor had I simply given him the benefit of the doubt. I was ashamed of myself, too ashamed even to say anything. But I felt a weight lift off my shoulders as we headed off to don our masks and throw a bunch of water balloons at the kids gathered outside.

As I did so, I remembered another friend whose involvement that day was similarly commuted. She did tons of work and gave plenty of support, but avoided the direct engagement with grief that my raw psyche demanded. Yet somehow, because I had interacted with her much more frequently in the interim, I had made my quiet peace with her and generously forgiven what I imagined to be an egregious unkindness. At the same time, my shame at such pettiness meant that this transaction happened only in secret—that the balance sheet in my heart had been reconciled without any outside acknowledgment. So I had never inquired or even considered what must have been an exceedingly painful reason for her absence, nor did it seem kind or fair to do so now.

As I revisited these memories, I also called to mind a professional colleague and fellow church attendee who took the time to attend a memorial service held in the garden outside our home. I remembered where I was standing on the flagstone walkway as he gave me advice about dealing with keepsakes and boxes full of memories. At the time, it seemed completely out of context: he was clearly reflecting on the loss of his parents, who had both died only months earlier after many long years and had left him with a house packed full of their many possessions, prized and otherwise. In fact, he had only recently finished sorting their things and selling off this faraway house. Somehow, the contrast between a houseful of a lifetime of memories and shared experiences and a collection of tiny clothes and keepsakes that fit into a couple of boxes was too much for me to bear. The disparity seemed to mock me, and I found some way to give the appearance of listening before I offered thin thanks and excused myself from the conversation. And I remembered how I had found myself in another city, months later, gustily complaining about this to some friends, except this time I realized that in spite of my repeated complaints about his lack of assistance to me in my grief, I had never really helped him in his. This I realized with a kind of shame and remorse that took my breath away, and I still haven't had the courage to apologize to him for my lack of support in his grief.

It is a grace to be relieved of the burden of my own preoccupation with myself, but it is painful, too. When I'm not the center of the universe, I can't allow myself to be only and always a recipient of kindness, but must realize that I too am a participant in this human drama, this dance between life and death, this network of conjoined lives and this sharing of pain and grief. If one monkey has gotten off my back, I've traded him for another one. The new one expects more of me, sure, but he's at least less self-absorbed, demanding, and shallow. He recognizes that there are other people in the world—people with their own struggles and challenges and grief, people whom I can help, just as they have helped me. This monkey is a little more human than the one who came before, and I grudgingly accept his challenge to give something back.

Friendship

Before, during, and after this grand ordeal of life and death, we have been blessed with a bunch of help in practical matters and in the intangible support that we soak up like a sponge. The combination is powerful.

There are the friends who, while we were still pregnant, bought us two car seats.

This was a dangerous move, for we were quite uncertain about the prospects for our children, and therefore likely to be hurt by this gesture. So they did this with great trepidation, and very tentatively told us about it. With equal gravity we thanked them and quietly dared to hope that we would have use for two car seats. For several weeks we considered the best course of action, finally inviting them to bring over one seat and teach us to install it. The second seat they graciously stored in the corner of their one-bedroom apartment, a symbol of hope that they kept for us.

When we were finally told that we could bring our son home, we informed them and they delivered it to the long-term care facility, where we were spending our days and nights. The journey down the elevator to the parking garage to install the seat was equal parts trepidation and joy, and my friend later told me that it was one of the best days of his life. I know it was one of mine.

And on the day after the dark night, when the sun's bright light was so painful, that same seat sat empty and silent. Another friend understood completely when I asked her to take it from us. Without hesitation or comment, she watched me duck into the car to push the seat-belt button that released it from its tight grasp. She put it in her own car, then stored it in her attic to wait until we were ready to see it again.

These are the friendships that we need: quiet, strong, supportive. There were faraway friends who sent gifts and boxes of clothes, and nearby friends who sorted it all out for us. Friends who sent simple emails, and friends who pulled weeds in the garden. Friends who sent money, and friends who brought us sandwiches at the hospital. A friend who carefully composed a meal of comfort food (sausages and tater tots, with frosting-dipped cookies for dessert, all washed down with soda), and a friend who sewed a tiny black funeral dress for our daughter. Friends who read our ramblings, friends who listened to our questions, and friends who absorbed our vague and undirected anger. When we are silent, they know that does not mean we have completed our grief, and when we say too much, they know we are being cathartic.

In the biblical story of Job, just after God wrecked Job's life on a dare, Job's friends visit in two waves, with two very different purposes. In the second wave, the friends stood before Job, quoting perfect orthodoxy and confidently explicating the mysteries of God with impeccable logic. This approach earned them the scorn of both Job and God, and of every reader forevermore.

But their first visit was more appropriate, and more appreciated. They came to their friend, who was laid out on the ground, unrecognizable for his extensive open sores, moaning in agony at his loss and pain. They came to this friend and they sat with him and wept.

Our friends near and far hold us, just as they keep our possessions. They hold our memories, and they share our pain. They speak a little, and they don't pester us with questions or theories of why bad things happen to people. They give us space, even and especially when they unintentionally infuriate us, or when we're just mad at the world. They wait and they pray and they wait some more, trusting that we know that they know, and know that they pray, and know that they wait. These friends hold us, they hold out hope for us, and they bear our burdens. They know we still need to laugh and to celebrate the other areas of our lives, and perhaps most important, they know that we need to wait with them in their disappointments and pains, too.

Avoidance

I'm faking it. I don't feel comfortable holding baby boys, and I'm barely able to admit it, even to my wife. Girls are no problem, and I definitely engage with little boys, if with a good dose of internal prodding. It's not like I ignore baby boys, either. I'll smile and coo and admire them and pat their heads and grab their plump bellies. I'd like to think this is because I'm simply programmed to leave little boys lying: to speak to them and to otherwise engage them, but to only touch them without picking them up, as I did with Will for the first month of his life. But in the end, I don't think this is the real reason for my obvious avoidance.

On a couple of occasions I've crossed the threshold toward engagement with baby boys, only to experience disconcerting results.

The first time, I held on far too long, the clock turning toward two hours before his mother finally, graciously hinted her way to her son's release. Once I got started, I couldn't stop. I rationalized that he had fallen asleep, and I shouldn't wake him, but the truth lay deeper than that. I held him quietly, his plump, perfect face refracted by the tears that welled—but didn't fall—from my eyes. I held him to recall what it felt like to hold my son, God forgive me.

On another occasion I carried a boy, who was about eighteen months old. *Borderline baby—a toddler, really,* I thought. *I'll be fine.* But it was weird, and I imagined that his mother was uncomfortable as I cradled his head in the way that isn't quite normal for a kid that big, and is certainly inappropriate for someone who's just a friend. *Once a kid can hold his own head upright, you don't stroke his hair unless you're related, knucklehead. Keep it together!*

With a newborn on a busy night at a noisy party, I again realized I was acting strangely . . . too slow or something, too deliberate, with too much thought in my eyes. Could they tell I was feeling him breathe? That I was thinking about death? That I was wondering how long it will be before a male infant is just a baby, and not my son?

This is hard to admit. I feel like the Grim Reaper or something, like I'm scarred for life, irreparably damaged. I'm glad I held my boy on that awful morning when the sun still shone.

I wouldn't do it differently, not a bit. But I'm afraid my arms will never be the same.

Sunshine

The onset of warm July days has coincided with a new awareness of our daughter's personality: she is bright, silly, frivolous, affectionate, outspoken (though nonverbal), and adventurous. In a word, she is a goofball.

She contrasts with her dad, weighted as he is with worry and sadness, distracted with the details of several part-time jobs, preoccupied with borrowing troubles from the other side of the world, and who spends a fair bit of time pouring dark thoughts into this black laptop; she races through the world in a shaft of light, completely blind to the anxieties all around her.

She's not perfect, of course. Just today, she repeatedly approached a forbidden object on a table until the temptation was removed, whereupon she flipped the table over, breaking it. But when she's not crying or screaming or making a mess, she is displaying nearly all her teeth in a wide grin. Quick to laugh, she often throws her head back to squint through slits and guffaws until her sides shake. After the table incident today, her mother was dispatching a few flies that had gathered in a window, likely drawn by the girl's aromatic diaper pail or her collection of food that accumulates on the floor with every meal. And for some reason that escaped us, every swat would result in loud gales of laughter—even when the swats were pointlessly delivered to the wall or ceiling, the fits of laughter would continue. She's just silly, I guess. Or maybe sadistic.

But with such hospitable weather, she accompanies me on runs, quietly rolling along in the jogging stroller without comment or complaint. When we're done, she cycles through ascents and descents of the stairs outside our apartment, frequently stopping midway to give herself a tiny round of applause and prompting the same from anyone watching. She loves to stomp her wet feet on the deck around the pool, jumping into the water again and again. And she is always eager to see the dogs that live next door, as evidenced by her running toward them with her mouth open, panting out the baby sign language for *dog*.

Back in our apartment, she's developing a visible affection for me, sharing her wet pacifier and the bites of food she may be eating. The other day I was awakened to my first, second, and third kisses from her, all delivered very wet and very much full on the lips. (I waited until she was looking the other way before wiping the slobber off my face.) After she wakes up from a nap, she'll bury her head into my chest and let me rub her back as she transitions into the world of wakefulness, finally letting me know she's ready to go by rearing her head back to grin at me and tickle me. She's invented her own sign language for *music* (it looks a little like the motions for "Itsy-Bitsy Spider"), twisting her hands in the air and sometimes moving her hips in a kind of rudimentary dance.

When I think of her now, she's staggering across the room to give me a big hug, climbing into my lap, and furrowing her eyebrows to deliver an earnest, extended monologue of obvious importance, but whose words are completely unintelligible. In fact, I often theorize that she's just making the sounds as a conversational placeholder, a down payment until the day when she can enlighten me about her bright vision of the world.

I'm sure that someday soon I'll be lecturing her, telling her that life is not a game, and that she needs to settle down and get stuff done. But for now, it is a blessing to have this living, breathing reminder that life doesn't need to be as burdensome as I often make it. That the burdens of this world are there for us to bear, but that we can choose to lay them aside, even if it's only for a tiny hug.

Qoheleth

Yesterday I dug a big hole. It took several hours to dig, and just a few minutes to fill back in. A hole that was almost completely pointless, come to think of it.

Though admired by many for its attractive South Seas ethos and its effective barrier to the prying eyes of our neighbors, I've learned the dark side of bamboo. It's incredibly invasive, spreading horizontal roots in every direction. Its thick roots lie anywhere between three inches and three feet below the surface, and pop through the crust of hard-packed earth, dirt mixed with rock, and even packed asphalt, sending up full-sized shoots that tower high into the sky in a matter of days. This thick network of roots is a challenge to pick and hack through as the digger tries to follow it back to its source.

Yesterday, the small shoot that poked through the flower bed turned out to be connected to a long, ropy root that went progressively deeper, until it disappeared under the thick subterranean concrete wall that had been built to contain it. After following the root all the way to where it disappeared under the wall's footing, my only recourse was to spitefully chop it off at that point. As I filled the hole back in, I smirked with the realization that the root would come back stronger than before, and that someone—me or a later resident—would be digging up the same root in the same spot at some point again in the future.

In this moment, I wipe my sweat with the back of my glove and call such reality "job security," but the experience hearkens back to words I heard on Sunday morning. Words attributed to a writer who claimed to be one of the sons of the mighty Jewish king, David. A writer who referred to himself as "Qoheleth," often translated *teacher* or *preacher*, which modern scholars have inexplicably translated with the strange term *Ecclesiastes*. This ancient book serves as a counterpoint to the more black-and-white, cause-and-effect wisdom found in biblical books like Proverbs. A unique part of the Hebrew Bible, Ecclesiastes talks about life and death and meaning with the bluntest of treatments, offering a none-too-rosy view of humanity:

> So I reflected on all this and concluded that the righteous and the wise and what they do are in God's hands, but no one knows whether love or hate awaits them. All share a common destiny—the righteous and the wicked, the good and the bad, the clean and the unclean, those who offer sacrifices and those who do not.
>
> As it is with the good, so with the sinful; as it is with those who take oaths, so with those who are afraid to take them.
>
> This is the evil in everything that happens under the sun: The same destiny overtakes all. The hearts of people, moreover, are full of evil and there is madness in their hearts while they live, and afterward they join the dead. Anyone who is among the living has hope—even a live dog is better off than a dead lion!
>
> For the living know that they will die, but the dead know nothing; they have no further reward, and even their name is forgotten. Their love, their hate and their jealousy have long since vanished; never again will they have a part in anything that happens under the sun.
>
> Go, eat your food with gladness, and drink your wine with a joyful heart, for God has already approved what you do. Always be clothed in white, and always anoint your head with oil. Enjoy life with your wife, whom you love, all the days of this meaningless life that God has given you under

the sun—all your meaningless days. For this is your lot in life and in your toilsome labor under the sun. Whatever your hand finds to do, do it with all your might, for in the realm of the dead, where you are going, there is neither working nor planning nor knowledge nor wisdom.

I have seen something else under the sun: The race is not to the swift or the battle to the strong, nor does food come to the wise or wealth to the brilliant or favor to the learned; but time and chance happen to them all.

Moreover, no one knows when their hour will come: As fish are caught in a cruel net, or birds are taken in a snare, so people are trapped by evil times that fall unexpectedly upon them.

Ecclesiastes 9:1–12

Depressing, yes. And yet it seems somehow freeing, too. So many of the messages of our culture—from *Sesame Street* to motivational speakers to films, music, and even sermons preached in churches—are to "make your mark" or "make a difference" (which we're generally meant to understand as beneficial, rather than, say, starting a forest fire or something), to "think positive" (the tortured grammar of which is never noticed), or to expect happiness and prosperity when we get our lives in proper order (which is the general message of books like Proverbs).

It seems to me there is real hope in this insight of Qoheleth: that this whole human project truly is circular. That the vast majority of us will live our lives and will be almost entirely forgotten in a few hundred years or less. Forgotten, even if we've lived our lives with utter earnestness and abundant energy, even if we've managed some small claim to fame, even if we've been mentioned in a sound bite, and even if our funeral service ends up being a crowded affair. Like headstones that fade and whose letters are eventually scoured to invisibility by wind and rain, our bodies and lives will be as dust—fertilizer for later generations, and eventual components of other plants and animals and people.

This can be depressing—I'm feeling a little heavy writing it just now—but there is freedom here, too. Once we realize we are all in this race together, making countless laps around the same track, we can slow down and enjoy the scenery. We can stop being so competitive, shoulders and elbows and hips jockeying for position, and get to know our fellow participants. Life is not a race, but an event, and one that is to be enjoyed and endured in proper turn.

Recently I found myself at a reunion and anniversary of a church I used to attend, and had a wonderful time. It was great to see so many old friends, and to feel their love, and to love them in return.

So, in the midst of this occasion, I was surprised to find myself so offended, and by such a well-intentioned person. Expressing compassion and sympathy over the loss of my son, he related a similar story of a family member whose infant son had developed an unexpected and terminal heart condition. The family traveled to a renowned hospital for treatment, and the boy survived surgery and recovered very nicely. And then, on the long drive home, the family car was involved in a serious traffic accident and the little boy died.

Feeling the weight of this loss, and the grief of the family, and the pain and waste of life, and the desperate questions they must have asked of God, I simply choked out an exasperated, "Oh, that is awful."

"Well," he offered brightly, "his mother had a really hard time for a while, but it became a really great testimony for the Lord, and many people were ministered to by her story."

Aghast, I just stared back, trying to think of something to say. "They must have had some serious questions for God, though, right?"

He shrugged. "But questions like those will only be answered *Someday*." His sibilance capitalized the word, and his head tilted out the italics to let me know he was talking about The Day of our Lord's Glorious Second Coming. "And besides, on that great day, we won't even care, will we?!" This last bit seeming not so much a question as an exhortation to right thinking.

But it does matter, doesn't it? Doesn't this whole existential drama have some meaning? Don't our lives matter? If not, then why has God put us on this planet, but for some kind of cruel prelude for heaven?

But we do have bodies, and appetites and children. We do feel pain, and suffer and ask questions. All of this is real and must be important or we wouldn't be doing it. With more courage and decorum, my question to my friend would have been, Then why does God leave us on the planet? If it's all about heaven and life after death, then why make us wait? Or, at the very least, why have us feel pain and suffer?

False dichotomy though it may be, I'd much rather embrace the circularity and meaninglessness of Qoheleth than to succumb to the mind-numbing ravages of modern dualism, where my pain and pleasure are equally unimportant. My pain is real, and my pleasure, too. Both are fleeting, but they are not to be denied, by me or by my Maker.

Frozen

I don't normally remember people's names, but one Sunday afternoon I was at a Target in a neighboring suburb. There, I saw a face, and my brain reflexively said *Joe*. I looked again for several seconds before I realized he was a man from our childbirth class. I said his name inside my head again, and the name *Allison* also popped up. So I looked around him and, sure enough, there was his wife.

My heart moved toward them, for they were kind folks, a couple who had made a point of connecting with us during the class, in spite of our obvious distance. Because we knew our pregnancy had many complications, and that our children had many challenges, we were guarded about what we shared. We mentioned that my wife was on bed rest, but we spoke not a word about our son's heart problems, cleft features, and extremely small size. To talk about those things that constituted some of the very worst fears for any parent seemed unkind, and so we kept the secrets to ourselves and spared our new friends the worry that we faced.

Looking back, I see too that we desperately wanted a place where we could be "normal," where we could talk about the first-order worries of parenting: pregnancy and birth, breast-feeding and naps, life adjustments and sleeplessness, the ordinary fear of what it means to be responsible for the life and development of another person. So for those three hours on Sunday evenings, we would pretend that these were our only concerns, and save the life-and-death stuff for the other 165 hours of our week.

Somehow, through all the smoke and mirrors, Allison and Joe had connected with us, and had continued the connection after we all became first-time parents. A few months after our twins were born, and after everyone else's kids were safely home and growing, my wife sent an email and a photo to our whole childbirth class. A few of the families replied, but Allison and Joe's words seemed more sincere somehow, and more empathetic. They offered to come by and bring a meal. This was a generous gesture, given the fact they were caring for their own brand-new daughter.

After Will died, my wife wrote another email to the group. It seemed unkind to reflect the reality that the lives of our children were so fragile, but we wanted to inform those who had been so supportive and also concerned. Once again,

Allison and Joe's reply was simple and sincere, full of love and empathy and understanding.

So when I saw them in the store, one might imagine I would rush to them, thank them for their kindness, and gush over their daughter and let them gush over ours. But that's not what happened. Instead, the very second I saw them, I knew I could not talk to them. I put my head down and powered my cart right past them, hoping they wouldn't see me, and knowing that if they did, I'd keep right on going. If they shouted my name, I'd pretend I didn't hear them.

Once I was past them, I took a quick left down an aisle to grab a bottle of dishwashing detergent and then hurried to the cash register. As the nice man scanned each of my items and put them into bags, I glanced up furtively, my eyes filling with tears. I grabbed my receipt and rushed to the car, looking over my shoulder the whole time and promising myself I'd only ever go to the Target right by my house in the future. Finally, with the cart returned to the nearby corral, Ella buckled in, and the car out of the lot, I let the tears flow as I drove back home.

Even now, weeks later, I can't understand what was so unbearable about saying hello. I know they would have been exceedingly gracious, and would probably not have said any more about Will's death than, We're so sorry, or some other kind comment. I have no doubt they would have loved Ella, and celebrated her, and that we would have shared some of the joys and challenges of parenting. I would have asked Allison if she was back to work at the magazine, and Joe if he still had time to race his bicycle. It would have been nice, but it would have been unbearable for me.

Perhaps I didn't want to think about it. I didn't want to miss him. Perhaps I wanted to pretend we hadn't been through that whirlwind. I didn't want to see their cute baby and remember that our "two" had become "one." I didn't want to think about the relative calm of their life, to stare enviously across the fence at what I imagined to be lush green grass on the other side. Sometimes I miss him so much that I don't want to think about it, don't want to talk about it. I just want to confide in my wife, who knows what it means when I say, "I just miss him."

Redemption

While I'm mostly in my head with this process of grief, writing about it and talking about it occasionally, my wife is much more circumspect. Hesitant to say much, she only rarely offers updates on her processing of this, and intense bits of wisdom (which I internalize and then appropriate in my conversations and writing). But more than that, she's remarkably practical, integrated, holistic and courageous in her moving forward: a few weeks after our son died, she returned to work as a labor and delivery nurse, helping other women give birth and welcome their children into the world. Patients with perfectly healthy babies and storybook endings, patients who are insolent and demanding as they endure the difficulty of childbirth, and many patients with high-risk pregnancies and at-risk babies.

Most of her experiences are strictly confidential. Laws govern the sharing of information about families, but this laboratory for grief is quite intense, and stuff often spills out as I drive her home, as she reflects on coming alongside families who have grave worries about relatively innocuous complications, and who ultimately breathe a deep sigh of relief and embrace their child when she is pronounced "perfectly healthy."

Stacy talks about helping fearful new moms with the normal adjustments to motherhood, never mentioning the fact that, though quite real and understandable, these fears are related to babies who will thrive and have absolutely no significant difficulties. She confides about helping the mother of twins, one of whom is a hypoplastic left heart patient, just like our son. After working with the family all day, she's forced to stammer out a pointedly truncated personal history when an overly helpful and only partially informed intern obstetrician offers, "You should talk to your nurse—she had twins, and one of them was a cardiac patient!"

Another mother of twins finds out that the second of her twins has a cleft palate when the pediatricians holler across the room, "You know that one of your twins has a cleft palate, right? Well, this one does, too." And my wife stays after her shift to make sure this mother is aware of the resources available for pumping breast milk and delivering it via a special bottle. Fortunately or unfortunately, the mother is well acquainted with all this, her first child being born with a cleft palate as well. In fact, the mother knows the world-renowned plastic surgeon, who practices at the children's hospital too—the same one whom we visited when our son was alive.

Of course, kindness and confidentiality prevent my wife from sharing this information. She doesn't share much of anything, really. How helpful would it be to begin a sympathetic narrative, only to be forced to disclose the fact that the patient died? So the redemption is quiet and kind, an unspoken empathy that I imagine is unconsciously and eagerly absorbed by the new and fearful parent, who will not wonder until later—if ever—why this nurse was so concerned, so empathetic, so engaged with their worry and grief. Why this nurse came in on her day off "just to check in" and why she possessed so much specialized knowledge about Haberman Feeders and fortified breast milk. The new parents won't know that the price paid for such engagement includes fitful, quiet car rides home, and anxious adjustments back to the normality of home life and bedtimes and TV. They won't know that the beautiful baby waiting for her in the car is also a reminder of a life lost. And the parents won't know that the benefit of such painful engagement is ultimately freedom; the working out of a salvation from self-condemnation and guilt and worry and grief.

Reminders

Ten months after the death of our son, our lives are largely normal. We work and exercise and cook and attend church and take our daughter to the playground. We travel and talk on the phone and laugh and watch television and enjoy friendships and clean the house (well, occasionally). New acquaintances might not even know what we've been through, and we don't usually feel the need to fill them in.

Indeed, we're *strong* in many ways—maybe stronger than we've ever been. And then, suddenly and surprisingly, we find ourselves weak in ways we don't even understand. We'll realize we are unexplainably anxious, or sad, or bitter, or conflicted, or just feeling very tired. So we take the time to comb over the details of the day and find the source of our malaise.

Recently we did some self-examination to understand why the mere mention of his name—Will Stavlund—evokes so much emotion. It is certainly not what is said about him (which is always respectful or even laudatory), but just that his name is invoked. Our insights here aren't clear or comprehensive, but seem twofold:

There's an element of selfishness—that it's our name to speak, and not others', even those whom we love and who speak well of him. This is obviously nonsensical, as deep in our hearts we'd love to see every person on the planet know him and honor him and speak his name with reverence. Yet at the same time we'd like to corner the market on his existence and persona and reputation—we selfishly feel that he belongs to us.

But even more pointedly, his name reminds us that he was real, and the reality of his life causes us pain, and so we tend to avoid it. I fully recognize the depth of this conundrum: I think about him every day, and I write about him several times a week. But I tend to think and write about him as an abstracted, impersonal idea. He, the Platonic form of a Departed Son, and me, the idealized image of a Grieving Father. But I don't tend to think about our undersized, unborn, unnamed baby, the source and subject of much earnest prayer for healing and for life.

Not *Will*, my son who used to fit into these hands, who used to slowly blink his beautiful eyes at mine, who used to fall asleep on my shoulder and breathe on my neck.

Not *William*, a handsome boy despite being burdened with his father's large forehead, prominent eyebrows, and largish ears.

Not *Will Stavlund*, who preferred to have a fresh, pristine diaper before he would have a bowel movement, thank you very much.

Not *William Addison Stavlund*, the hanging branch on my family tree.

Not *Will*, the baby who would become a boy, and a man.

So we hear his name, and we choke, and we reconnoiter and talk about our stormy feelings and find the truth in our swirling circumstances. In so doing, we realize it is better this way, a grace to have him taken so quickly. It is better that he's gone, and has moved on into the fullness of himself. It is selfish for us to hang on to him in one sense, and to deny his reality in another.

We unpack an inexplicably tumultuous day and realize that the song sung at church was also sung at the funeral. Which is fine—beautiful and honoring, truly—but also grabs at our ears and squeezes ever so slightly. So many details like this one to be identified, addressed, and reconciled.

We need to make our peace with such reminders, lest we be forever encumbered.

We need to accept such remembrances as the hopeful promises they are.

We need to remember that there were funerals before our iconic Funeral, and there will be funerals after.

We need to remember that these songs are valuable precisely because they belong to everyone, in the midst of myriad experiences and life transitions.

We need to find the joy and the pain in the singing of these songs, now and in the future.

And campy though it is, we struggle with the kind euphemisms that are at our disposal. They are gentle and nice, but they seem to allow us too much denial of our reality. My wife was cruising through a day recently, answering an email request for information. The email was kind and gracious and understanding, a considerate note regarding a thoughtful memorial from the mother of another hypoplastic left heart baby. The sensitive mother whose son also died used gentle words like "passed" or "left us" or "departed." My wife was tempted to respond in this way, but instead forced herself to key in the four letters: "*died* September 12, 2006." The letters that don't lie, or pretend that he's only gone for a little while, or that he'll be coming back. The four final letters that say he is gone, forever, leaving us with the pain of his absence, but also with the joy of his life, with the thankfulness that we were able to know him, and with gratitude that he was freed from the limitations of his body.

Final Push

Physicality

A couple of weeks ago, a friend offered a kind invitation to join him at an upcoming event. A fund-raiser had been organized in the form of a five-mile Fun Run and one-mile walk to support children's cardiac research and the families who go through the arduous journey of surgeries, recovery, and uncertainty. The event is named in honor of a little boy who had died of complications just before his second birthday, and was organized by the child's mother just a year after his death. My friend noted that the boy had suffered with the exact same heart condition as our son, and knowing that I used to be an avid runner, he thought to invite me along.

My wife and I quickly committed to participate, and so our training began. My days of running are long gone: when the pregnancy began almost two years ago, my motivation to run every day was replaced with a deep desire to ramp up my odd-job income and bank some cash, so I essentially put my running shoes in the closet. I've had a couple of relapses where I strung together several weeks of running, but the end result is that by replacing running with round-the-clock child care and a diet high in dairy products, I'm about thirty pounds heavier with only a memory of my former cardiovascular efficiency.

A sudden return to running in the heat of a Washington, DC summer is brutal indeed. Where I used to light out the door first thing in the morning to run for an hour or two every day, I now squeeze runs between naps and meals, plodding behind a jogging stroller and occasionally communicating with my daughter between gasps to point out birds or bunnies or doggies. Yet even more than the familiar sense of depression and dread that comes with the memories of my former (imagined) glory, I'm now burdened with the memory of my son, whose own cardiovascular inefficiencies dwarfed my own.

With only a two-chambered heart and palliative re-plumbing of the major vessels and arteries around this vital organ, he was constantly struggling for breath. Even when he was given high concentrations of oxygen to breathe, the saturations of oxygen in his blood would never be higher than 85 percent, and were routinely in the 65–75 percent range. For comparison, I'm quite certain that even in my toughest workout or hardest push at the end of a marathon, my pulse-ox reading would never have been below 90 percent. Home-care nurses and medical professionals unfamiliar with his condition would routinely fight panic as they checked and rechecked the monitoring equipment and quizzed us before finally accepting that these readings were not inaccurate, his mother and I were not incompetent, and he didn't need to be immediately rushed to the hospital by ambulance.

What this meant was that our little boy was blue. Many of the babies in the cardiac unit were, such that we stopped even noticing his hue. Even now, I can click over to the photo of Will and his sister on my computer desktop and see the remarkable difference in their skin tone. She, flush and fat and smiling, and he, thin and straining, skin tinged with blue and with visible veins on his forehead. Yet this wasn't something I really noticed when he was alive. He was just Will, and she was Ella. That was normal.

Remembering all this now while on a run, I'm impetuously inspired to push myself exceedingly hard—to run full bore up every hill in our neighborhood, to scheme a plan to win the race with my will alone, to perhaps stop training so I can suffer all the more on that hot Saturday morning, to gut out the whole five miles with only the inspiration of my son. After all, even with my most supreme athletic effort, I won't reach the level of cardiac output that Will experienced while he was sleeping or resting. Even if I pushed five strollers through ten miles of mud while breathing around a mouthful of water, I wouldn't be as coordinated or dedicated as he was when he would take an ounce of milk by bottle. *No matter what I do, I'll never be blue.* So why not just blast through those five miles, flat out, as a way to honor him and identify with him?

That of course would be monumentally stupid, really. I'll not honor him by having a cardiac event of my own, or by heroically huffing past nice people at a *Fun* Run, or by blasting through the course, bravado firmly in place. It ought to be enough that I remember him while I push his sister's stroller, that I celebrate her life, that I honor the freedom she and I now enjoy to leave the house and see the world outside, that I remain forever humbled by his heroism. It ought to be enough that I join with other families who have suffered similar loss.

But something deep inside me wants to avoid this connection with others. I'd rather be an isolated individual, an unfortunate victim of not only a rare heart condition but of the even more exclusive, silent club of people who came out on the wrong side of the percentages. The health-care mail we still receive features stories of cardiac anomalies in newborns, of families in crisis, and of ultra-competent surgeons, each of whom find healing and happiness and success, respectively—perfectly happy endings. And this is as it should be. No one knows more than I do that those who are faced with such frightening prognoses need hope, and that the hospitals that help them are in desperate need of funding.

Yet in spite of my envy at their better outcomes, I acknowledge with much weariness and loneliness that the story of my son isn't one that will be useful in any way, except possibly as a salve for someone else who has suffered loss. No one's talking about The Amazing Will at the children's hospital, because it would be utter cruelty to answer a parent's question about his outcome with any honesty. Maybe his story will offer some cold comfort to a family that finds themselves on the other side, headed back to the car with an empty stroller, but it should be a secret until that dark day.

In the meantime, I need to put myself in community with others. That is where healing happens, where burdens are shared, where faith is restored. But if misery loves company, it isn't a very good friend either. On the few occasions I've gathered with other bereaved families, everyone is awkward and uncomfortable. For all the ways we may feel unreasonably isolated, marginalized, or even silenced, we don't have much to say when we see one another.

"It is hard" certainly communicates something significant, and words are probably extraneous anyway. But there is also a palpable sense of desperate self-pity in the air, and it is distasteful. My own self-pity is familiar and common—the taste that lives inside my mouth, unnamed and unnoticed. But when I get a whiff of someone else's self-pity, I am repulsed. When I smell my self-pity drifting back over myself, I'm nauseated. So I tend to avoid such interactions. "Those people are really miserable," I say with pained irony.

Maybe salvation comes in sharing. I share my pain, blow the self-pity out of my mouth, loosen my grip on the control of the experiences of myself and my family, and stop wielding my grief against other folks—both those who are similarly bereaved and those who are unafflicted. In the same way, my neighbors can share their pain, and their experiences, and allow both to soften me. Maybe we really can learn to share our burdens, mourn with those who mourn, and celebrate with those who celebrate.

Someday I want to be completely, wholeheartedly happy for those who find themselves pregnant, and whose kids run and play in the playground—those families whose good health is enjoyed in beautiful, blissful ignorance. I don't want to always compare them to me, to jockey for position, to rank our pains and weaknesses and naiveté. I don't want to assume they haven't suffered, not like me. I want to accept people at face value while at the same time realizing that what lies behind our faces is even more important.

When we first got the news that the lives of our twins were hanging in the balance in utero, a decision came to me. If we lost them, I would get a tattoo of some kind to remember them, to honor them, to express through pained flesh what I was feeling inside. Since that time, I must have lost my nerve, for I rarely think about designing an image and visiting a tattoo parlor. But as I look forward to the race in a few days, I think that I might like to take a permanent pen and mark Will's name on my flesh to tell the world something about my pain. However, that seems selfish and overly demonstrative, so I hedge my bet and consider writing both his name and the name of the boy whose memory the event honors. I think about this, but it doesn't seem right either—it seems disrespectful toward his parents, for I project my own tendencies and imagine that they want to possess their son's memory and the expression of his life. But this cannot be. Only a year after his death, they have organized this fund-raiser, effectively sharing him with the world. In this way, they are already sharing their son, letting go, redeeming their grief. In this way, they shine a beacon of light and hope for me.

Anniversary

Today is Friday, July 13. In and of itself, this doesn't worry me or scare me at all. I might be superstitious, but I'm not *that* superstitious. The only real significance of today is yesterday. I looked at the clock on the wall this afternoon and realized I missed yesterday. Will died on the 12th, and for some reason I feel the need to remember that each and every month. And this month I was thinking about it around the 7th and 8th, and after that I guess I forgot.

As soon as I realized I had missed the 12th, I tried to catch my breath and said something about it to my wife. She was understanding in her empathy, but resolute in her assessment. "It's good that you forgot that day," she said, but under my redirect, she also confessed that she herself had remembered.

"That's easy for you to say." I was more envious than accusatory.

I paced through the kitchen before I stabilized myself against the countertop and tried to recall what I had done the day before. Some of the pieces were in place, but others were reluctant to fall out of my memory. Finally it all came together. There was an early wake-up with the baby, and subsequently a handoff of Ella to my wife, followed by three huge loads of laundry at the laundromat up the hill—a three-hour, thirty-dollar day. Then a quick shower, a haircut across town, lunch at home, then yard work for a few hours. This followed by a brief family swim in the pool, then a quick trip to the supermarket to pick up a few things for a dinner meeting at our place. And finally a few friends came by for BLTs made with our fresh tomatoes, after which we talked about following Jesus.

It was a good day, or so I thought. Not a waste, not by my normal measure. But because I didn't remember this sad event, didn't pause for a moment of pained reflection, didn't raise a beverage or a prayer in his memory, I had somehow failed on that day. I was a bad parent because, when my hair stylist asked about our grief, I didn't mention the fact that our son had died exactly ten months earlier—I didn't offer that point of precision. Because I forgot to punish myself with the memory of that dark day, a singular event had passed through my hands, never to be repeated. I wished I could turn back the clock so that I could transform a relatively happy, productive day into a more shadowy version of itself.

My wife must be right. It's not a good or reasonable goal that I anticipate and mark every monthly anniversary, to treat the twelfth like it's a due date for some big bill. It's good to forget some of these dark details, to move on, to find a measure of productivity and happiness, and to live for the future instead of in the past. But for some reason, this seems unnatural, and disrespectful.

Crossing the Line

Race

The day I had been working toward was bright and warm, but not oppressively hot. We met up with several friends who were joining us, talking for a minute before we made our way to the starting line.

The first mile of the course was lined with large plastic traffic cones spaced several yards apart, each bearing the image of a baby with dates printed below. As I started to notice this memorial, Will's face flashed by my right elbow, and I choked. Shaking off the tears and forcing myself to breathe, I plowed ahead with my eyes fixed on the horizon. When after several minutes I had safely avoided a sobbing, teary-eyed crash into a tree and regained my composure, I noticed there were many, many more memorials. Running through this gauntlet of grief reminded me that every one of these images represented another very difficult life cut (tragically? mercifully?) short, another family buried in questions, another dad trying to find his way forward. The accumulation of this collective angst was a weight too great to bear, and so I was glad to see that eventually the memorials ended, giving way to a shady gravel path through the woods.

There, I found a cadence and entered into the familiar realm of hypoxia and cardiac inefficiency—to find that sharp edge of discomfort—and push on and on and on. This is a realm I had nearly forgotten, but which greeted me like an old companion: that space between urgent effort and relaxation, between a celebration of and a denial of one's own flesh, between life and (what feels like) death.

There, I thought of my son, who dwelt in this very place every minute of every day. And when I was pressing through the heat and hills of the last mile, I kept him firmly in my mind. Yes, I felt like stopping and lying down—very much, and very urgently—but I also remembered I can keep going, as long as I don't stumble and crash. This is a strange place—dark and silent, mysterious and painful—but it is only temporary. I know I can keep pushing on. As I bore down for the last half mile, I experienced that old tunnel vision as I used most of the oxygen in my blood to move forward, until I finally crossed the finish line, feeling all at once that I was very constrained and very free.

Letting the Sun Shine

It is an August Saturday that hearkens toward the fall, the morning after a break from a week of oppressive 100-degree Washington, DC heat. I was shocked this morning to find that the heat is gone, replaced with a cool 70-degree breeze. Better yet, the smoggy haze that gets trapped by temperature inversion is gone too, replaced with clear blue skies.

So I'm sitting out on the porch in the morning, checking email with my laptop computer while my daughter naps inside. Though I've stopped noticing it, to my right is an empty container of dry dirt. Months ago in the church meeting where I shared some thoughts about the weakness of God and Jesus' metaphor of daylilies, we actually planted daylilies so that we could have an ongoing reminder of God's concern for us. I was nervous to take mine home—even more nervous than when we brought our two kids home. Before they were born, I had dreams that our children would die of our neglect. Of course, the reality of children brought with it the chagrined awareness of their constant reminders: it would be hard to let a child go hungry or be uncomfortable, equipped as they are with powerful lungs and vocal cords. What I learned was that if a child needed anything, she or he would go ahead and sound an alarm. No one was going to go quietly.

But plants don't have vocal cords. I was worried; I've allowed many plants to die before and so I knew I needed a strategy. Should I try to develop a daily habit of watering the bulb? Should I research the optimal growing environment and orchestrate the surroundings accordingly? Should I create a scenario of mutual dependence between me and the plant? In the end, I decided the best plan was to approximate a kind of God-centered growing environment. I put the plant in a spot on our porch where it would get sun in the cool morning, shade in the hot afternoon, and water anytime it rained. I hedged my bet by poking holes in the bottom of the container to prevent an abundance of rain from drowning the plant, and by pouring a little water into the dirt anytime I noticed it was dry.

So I was relieved when, after what seemed like a long period of inactivity, a tiny shoot breached the shell of the bulb, heading skyward. The shoot became a stalk, and the stalk started to develop a bud at the top. And then things got kind of quiet. Nothing much seemed to be happening, and I avoided panic by giving little drinks of water and hoping against hope that things were not as they seemed. Until several weeks later, when my daughter's tiny hand pulled the whole dry thing up out of the dirt and I had to admit that the flower was completely dead. Still, I haven't had the heart to go ahead and throw the dirt and crusty plant away.

But on this perfect Saturday, I'm reading an email a friend has sent out to one of our church's email lists. In it she celebrates this glorious day and offers some beautiful commentary about her daylily and its bright blossoms. The email includes these words from Jesus, and has several photos of the flower attached.

> Therefore I tell you, do not worry about your life, what you will eat or drink; or about your body, what you will wear. Is not life more than food, and the body more than clothes? Look at the birds of the air; they do not sow or reap or store away in barns, and yet your heavenly Father feeds them. Are you not much more valuable than they? Can any one of you by worrying add a single hour to your life?
>
> And why do you worry about clothes? See how the flowers of the field grow. They do not labor or spin. Yet I tell you that not even Solomon in all his splendor was dressed like one of these. If that is how God clothes the grass of the field, which is here today and tomorrow is thrown into the fire, will he not much more clothe you—you of little faith? So do not worry, saying, "What shall we eat?" or "What shall we drink?" or "What shall we wear?" For the pagans run after all these things, and your heavenly Father knows that you need them. But seek first his kingdom and his righteousness, and all these things will be given to you as well. Therefore do not worry about tomorrow, for tomorrow will worry about itself. Each day has enough trouble of its own.
>
> Matthew 6:25–34

Later in the day, I find a package that arrived the day before. It is from some generous folks who live far away, dear friends from a church of which we used to be a part. Inside the box, there is a very nice handwritten letter describing how they found a sculpture and how it immediately reminded them of us and so they simply had to send it to us. My heart sank as I pulled all of the packing and wrapping from the box and I saw it: a plaster piece depicting an angel carefully conveying a tiny baby upward. To my surprise, it was not flowery or soft or puffy or cheesy, as I often find such sentimental pieces. It was realistic, beautiful, with careful detail, evocatively gaunt faces and an obvious sense of movement. Only to me, no matter how many times I changed my viewing angle, it looked like the Grim Reaper taking a baby up to heaven.

It was a confluence of events that seemed as if it would push me toward despair and depression, to acting out in ways like casually dropping the statue off a balcony, or replying to the email list with the simple message, My flower lived for a few days, but then it died. But I didn't do any of these things. I felt sad, of course, and wondered if there was some reason why these things were coming together on the day before the monthly anniversary of my son's death. But I didn't do anything rash or say anything I'd regret.

Even after eleven months, my ability to see through any perspective but my own is still quite weak, but I'm at least beginning to see through the eyes of others. I see that my friend's email is written and sent with the best of intentions. It is, in fact, written in the face of my friend's own disappointments with life, composed with her own metaphorical dead flowers in mind. She knows not every lily will bloom and is not being triumphalist or celebratory in the face of my or anyone else's loss. And while she would even welcome my dissent and mourn with me, I'm aware that my indulgence of my own dark impulses would not be helpful to her or me or anyone else.

Too, this new perspective allows me to see that my friend's kind gift is one of pure love. He bought this expensive statue, and carefully packaged it, and shipped the package at no small expense. Even as I admit that I could never display it in our home, I feel loved and cared for and encouraged. And I worry about writing this—that my ungratefulness will be hurtful toward him, and that he won't understand how I can appreciate the gift and reject it at the same time.

I'm starting to see that selfishness is a side effect of grief, a kind of necessary self-protection. But it can also become self-destructive or, at the very least, isolating. My problem is, our good friends will bear with our selfishness for a very long time, perhaps longer than is healthy for us.

Fall

When you run through a Washington, DC summer, you literally slog around in shoes that are as wet with sweat as if you'd run through a long, shallow puddle. June, July, and August are stifling. But when August turns to September, the days of hot, hazy humidity begin to be interspersed with cool, breezy, bright days. The first few such days can feel downright chilly, though the same day would have felt warm in the spring.

Stepping out the door in shorts on one of these first fall mornings, it feels like a weight has been lifted off one's shoulders. The runner feels unburdened and light, and while you eventually do warm up, the sweat is not excessive, though you still go through the motions of brow-mopping. The pace is quicker, the runs last longer, and those who have been training for a fall marathon suddenly feel a tangible sense of hope and optimism as they realize they have more energy and endurance than they'd previously realized. *Maybe this thing won't kill me, after all.*

Looking back over the summer, I can see something similar in myself. I was living in a haze, but somehow the inner storm broke and I started to breathe more freely. I can still remember the thoughts and emotions that tortured me, but they are harder to access, and not nearly so pressing. I feel a strange kind of responsibility to store them in a safe place should I need to reference them again someday, yet they aren't so oppressive. Somehow, as scary as it feels, I'm beginning to wonder if I might be able to move on.

Time Machine

I'm living in three fall seasons simultaneously. As the morning air changes from humid to cool, and the leaves begin to turn the tiniest hues, and the grass starts to green again, and the days begin to shorten, I'm experiencing a shuffle of the three years that are past.

Two fall seasons ago, we were newly pregnant, filled with a mixture of fear and excitement. Our hopes and dreams had been fulfilled: we were the proud parents of eleven fertilized eggs, four of which continued to thrive over the next few days, until we visited the doctor's office to have the eggs transferred. We were more or less dutiful in our visit, expecting that we'd not get the news we desperately desired during the first few rounds of in-vitro fertilization, already steeling ourselves for the disappointing news as our doctor juggled the many variables we were up against. Moreover, our understanding was that the standard treatment protocol dictated two eggs be transferred in each of the six cycles of implanting that we had paid for.

So we were dumbfounded when the technician assisting us asked the monumental question, "So, how many eggs should we transfer?" The decision we thought had already been made by standard operating procedure was right in front of us, and we were struck speechless. We would need to decide quickly, and for keeps—the eggs were at their optimal point of growth, and any embryos not transferred today would need to be frozen immediately for future use. So we quizzed the technician about percentages and statistics and tried to weigh the slight chance that we'd get pregnant at all with the tiny chance that we'd be pregnant with twins. We were hoping for one, expecting zero, and barely imagining that we'd have two.

That fall was a season of excited disbelief and overwhelming hope. Our cup had been empty for ten years, and it was about to be very, very full, all at once. I vividly remember leaving the ultrasound suite, where the twin pregnancy was confirmed, and walking through a hallway of hugs from the doctors and staff at the infertility clinic, and taking the long way home so that we could stop at a notable high-end breakfast spot. We were sitting at a linen-covered table, brimming over with excitement. All around us sat the DC elite—politicians, pundits, and lawyers. Powerful people, and we commoners with overwhelming, life-altering news that was barely contained. I remember being torn between ordering an expensive, celebratory treat or cautiously splitting a thrifty dish to spare our bank account from the huge hit it was about to take. We were already parents, times two!

I'm also reliving last fall, when my exhaustion was tangible and my concerns were huge, but my hope was almost complete. We had been through so much, and our son had done so well. There were grave worries right in front of us, I knew: irritability in Will, poor circulation, lack of interest in feeding, and some ashen faces in the ultrasound suite of the cardiologist's office as they squinted to see his tiny aortic arch, which he was rapidly outgrowing. Will's health was declining and he needed to have his second surgery, very soon.

But he would get it soon. I was worried about all of these problems, but I couldn't dwell on them, even if I wanted to, because I couldn't afford to worry. We were under the care of the finest cardiac team we could find, and each member of that team was fully focused. So, I reasoned, I'd do my part, and they would do theirs. Besides, I was just too exhausted to notice much of what was happening all around me, too bleary-eyed to see his condition, too rushed to read the writing on the wall.

My perceptions had distilled down to this simplified version of reality: everyone wanted the same thing. Doctors, cardiologists, kidney doctors, surgeons, parents, family, friends, and even God wanted Will to live, and thrive, and squeal his way down the slide at the playground. So everyone would do what they could, and everything would be all right. And if it wasn't going to be all right, then all we could do was all we could do, anyway. We'd have to face the dark possibilities when they came, and not before. So I chose hope, because hope was the only option available.

This fall, hope seems distant, like the memory evoked by a yellowed photo from a family vacation. I can remember hope, can recognize it when it flits through my body, but I can't exactly recall what it was like to have so much hope. And even if I could go back, I'm not sure I would. I feel tired now too, but in a different way. I feel older, if not wiser. Weary of the world, and humbled at how it works, but steadier somehow. My emotions are more regulated, more consistent. I feel as if I have more endurance to see my way through whatever may come next.

My father used to teach me to moderate my expectations. He's no crusty cynic, but he's realistic. A pragmatist. "Most of what you worry about will not come to pass," he told me, again and again. He even cited a statistic about how only thirty percent of our worries ever come to fruition. So, basic economics would tell you to go ahead and press in to life, for most of the stuff you worry about won't happen. At the same time, my father tempered this realism with advice toward the other side of the balance: "If you plan for the worst, you'll often be pleasantly surprised." That advice I embraced, much more than the piece about worry. But as I got older, I thought better of "planning for the worst," deciding that it was leaving me flat; safe from the lows of disappointment, yes, but also lacking in excited expectation and the adventure of straining toward new goals just out of reach. I love my father, but I wasn't going to live in the middle anymore. I wanted to range out and soar through the highs and suffer through the lows. I'd pay the price of sadness, if I could get the benefit of hope.

Now I've lived through two years where I fostered hope against all the frightening things that might have happened. I'd see terrible news coming my way, and I'd think, *That can't be!* I'd pray, and dream, and nurture an expectation that I'd be delivered from my fears. And I'd sit in that place of hopeful waiting until I saw that my worst fears were, in fact, being realized.

And yet, somehow, hope is slowly filling in around the edges of my being. Fall can feel like something is leaving, something is dying, something is going dormant. But this fall, a bud of hope and a shoot of optimism are sprouting up. It scares me, to be honest.

Tree

As the one-year anniversary approaches, our kind friends are planning a get-together to find some space with each other, remember and celebrate. Our hope is that, one year later, we won't feel so much sadness or so much shock, and that we can reflect on the contributions our son made to our lives, to the ways in which we're better for knowing him, to the energy and hope he's given all of us, and to honor his memory.

The practice of these gatherings comes to us by a Sudanese friend who lost her daughter while she was pregnant with her third son. She found that, a year later, she was actually able to speak to her friends and to focus on the happier memories. We also read about it in Lauren Winner's book *Mudhouse Sabbath*, where she describes the Jewish prescription for the year following a death, and the way the family of the bereaved is helped by their community to navigate the first year of absence. And still another family who lost a child to HLHS told us about visiting, one year later, the cemetery where their son was buried, bringing with them a collection of kids who'd been friends of his. Their suggestion was to enact some kind of symbolic memorial—in their case, they released butterflies—to offer a tangible activity of remembrance for people to partake in.

Many people talk of planting a tree, and that makes sense to us, too. A tree being a symbol of life, and a permanent one at that. A tree being a place we can go and visit with our daughter, and a place for other people to go as well, if they desire.

My one hesitation is that the tree will die, too soon. This is unreasonable, I know. I have a friend who is a brilliant arborist, and he'll make sure the tree is of the proper species for the environment, and that the soil will support it, and he'll no doubt stop by to check on our particular tree. But my worry is deeper than that. It's founded in the fact that this whole project is one of uncertainty. And not just the planting of a tree; all of life is uncertain. I worry that the tree will die just as I worry that my daughter will die. Just as I worry that my wife or I might die, too. But what can we do about any of that? We can be vigilant, and careful. But trees and people die. Accepting that is the hard part. Stepping forward into that reality seems reckless.

One Year Later

The letter read at the anniversary gathering described above:

Dear Will,

First of all, I know it's kind of crazy for me to address you in this way. I'm not even sure you can hear me—or at least, I hope you have better things to do than attend to all of my worries and concerns. I hope you're working on something, somewhere, learning and growing and doing stuff. One thing I do know is that I certainly don't need to worry or wonder about whether you're working hard—you know all about effort and strength, my friend.

So, I know this is kind of a crazy, one-sided conversation, but it's definitely less crazy than me talking to myself, so there you go.

I love you, Will. Maybe more now than ever before. I certainly appreciate all you did in your short life, all you faced, all you overcame. I'm proud of you, my firstborn. At the same time, I'm so deeply sorry for all of your difficulty and pain and hardship, especially the stuff that we put you through. Surgeries, ventilators, stitches, bottles, therapies, examinations, blood draws, car rides, nasogastric tubes, baths, diapers, and general mishandling. I want you to know that I feel terrible for all of the pain that our choices brought you, but that we needed to do all of that, because we love you. We wanted to give you every chance at this life, because we love you. We chose to cause you pain, because we love you. I hope this makes more sense to you than it does to me.

And I miss you, Will. Every day, and in every way. Relieved as I am that you're not straining so hard inside such a weak vessel, I wish I could have you back. I want to hold you, and talk to you, to read you books and take you to the park, and to look and listen. You are an amazing person, Will. I miss hanging out with you. And—much as it breaks my heart to say it out loud— I'm glad you left us so quickly and decisively, because if I had any choice in the matter, I'd have never let you go.

And I wanted to thank you. For all you've given me, and us. But most especially, for your sister. Oh, Will, she is so beautiful, and full of life. She just learned to shake her head "no," and she does it a lot. She plays hard, and sleeps deep, and when I'm giving her a bottle and look into her eyes, I see you there, somehow.

Before you two were born, we prayed that we wouldn't lose both of you; that we'd get to know you both. Now I see that the answer to our prayer was your strength and self-sacrifice. Your perseverance allowed her to flourish, and her generosity allowed you to persevere. She still shares stuff, Will: stuffed animals, toys, clothes, hugs, chips, and drooly Cheerios. She shares so much, thanks to you.

Will, you gave us beauty—not only with your deep eyes, and your thick hair, and your love, and your strength, and your wide smile. You showed us that life, however difficult and wrought with pain it is, is still somehow filled with beauty. And you're still showing us, every day. I'm so grateful for you, and for your life.

> *With much love,*
> *Dad*

Theodicy

Though I'm feeling a mysterious lightness of being in recent days, some huge questions continue to hang over my head. One

that haunts me from over a year ago was shared by a friend
in response to a blog post I wrote when Will was in the ICU:

> My question is how to "trust" in such a seemingly capricious
> creature? What does it mean to trust in someone who actually
> doesn't promise to keep you safe or warm or even alive, who
> may or may not do anything about stuff and doesn't bother
> to tell you why? Is it supposed to be comforting that this guy
> wants to hang out with me in my troubles?
>
> I feel like I have no adequate theology for suffering, evil
> and injustice. They are just not explainable except to say that
> God shares our distaste for these things and is in the middle
> of a plan to redeem the world and end them all.

Another friend was writing on his own blog recently, reflecting on his view of God and trying to make sense of the
suffering of several friends: our family, but more pointedly,
his friend recently diagnosed with multiple sclerosis, and
another friend who was raped. "Indolent Bystander" is the
term he's coined, and it poignantly describes the conundrum
of theists everywhere. If God is all-powerful and good, why
then doesn't God intervene in such situations? Why doesn't
God reach down and help us with a "Magic Hand from the
Clouds" (another great turn of phrase by my friend)? If this
is a true view of the Divine, then God must be some kind of
distant deity, unconcerned about creation.

The truth I see both of my friends pushing me toward is
that this is a God of our own making. This Unmoved Mover,
this Prime Mover, this Watchmaker God was foisted upon
us by early Greek philosophers like Plato and Aristotle, and
by their Christian counterparts like Augustine. If God was
going to be translated into the cultural terms of the day—a
good and important project if there ever was one—then God
must be *pure reason*, perfect and far removed from humanity
(which must therefore be almost irredeemably flawed). There

must then be a gulf between God and us, and we must be unable to bridge that gulf. God must be omnipotent, just and right, and we must be evil.

To this view, the question has long been asked, Is this God kind, merciful and loving? So, onto this theological construction an addition was built, a defense of this God to counter the logical charges of God's unkindness and inaction in the face of human suffering: a *theodicy*. A mountain of literature has been produced, looking at this logical conundrum from many angles. Some theodicies tend toward God's involvement in the world, while others lean toward his stern justice, and still others suggest that our suffering is not *real* but only *apparent*, but all seem to engage this issue with the same basic terms: separation, elevation, and reason.

I'm wondering if there might be another way. Perhaps we created this need for theodicy when we separated God from ourselves. Good and right as it was to understand and translate the story of Christianity into the terms of the culture in the third century, why have we retained these categories and ideas for more than 1,500 years? What if we've gotten so accustomed to looking through these same lenses that we can't see any other way?

The God depicted in the Hebrew Bible (what is commonly referred to rather uncharitably as the Old Testament) is a God of passion and emotion. A God of great joy who also feels bitter heartbreak. An engaged figure who woos creation like a love-struck teenager. A God who doesn't offer rosy promises of happiness in the sweet by and by, but who connects with people to show them how to live in the here and now. A God who invites collaboration from people as the world is set aright, rather than sending them to some cosmic bleachers to wait for justice to come in one God-sized swoop.

At the same time, we see a God who, time and again, stands by and watches things go from bad to worse. A God who listens attentively as people complain about injustice, and whose occasional answers to those charges seem mostly unsatisfying to observers like us, but which somehow gave great comfort to the original recipients. God is "high and lifted up," to be sure, but the truly striking contribution of the Judaic vision of the Divine is the way in which God is moving in the warp and woof of our ordinary lives.

Of course, this image of God doesn't satisfy our modern lust for power. We don't want a God who walks with us; we want a God who solves our problems, gives us blessings, and settles all of our scores. We don't want a God who feels our pain; we want a God who can protect us in this life and provide for us in the hereafter. Above all, we don't want a God of *mystery*, but one who *makes sense*. But what if we're looking for something that God doesn't choose to give? What if we're asking questions that God won't answer, or whose answers we wouldn't understand anyway? What if we're barking up the wrong theological tree?

In her groundbreaking study of grief, Elisabeth Kübler-Ross described the final goal of grief as "acceptance"—that place where the bereaved can finally come to terms with their loss and begin to move on with their life. Over the past month, I've wondered if this stage might be better described as "exhaustion." The bereaved gets so tired of asking the same questions, so fatigued from feeling the same pain, so weary of waving the flag of memory for our loved one, so tired of feeding the delicate flame of remembrance, so bored of poring over the same emptiness, so exhausted of sustaining a protest against God, that he or she just gives up and goes along.

Now, this is not the same thing as defeat. In my experience, anyway, it is actually energizing and empowering to come to this place of exhaustion—to accept, finally, those things that cannot be changed, and those things that can be redeemed, and those things that lie in the mysterious space between.

To cease the struggle against that which cannot be changed, and to stop defending an understanding of God that's simply beyond our grasp. To root oneself in an understanding that God exists outside of our theologies, philosophies, and other theories. If someone needs to defend God, I'm sure there are many who are far more qualified, and I wish them well.

My questions remain:

Why did God allow Will's defects in the first place, when intervention was well within God's capacities?

Why did Will endure so many surgeries and sufferings, only to have his breath suddenly snuffed out?

Why does his loss hurt so much, and why can't I compartmentalize the pain?

Why can't I sequester the grief to some convenient part of my psyche so that I can take it out once a week, instead of having it bleed out, staining the fabric of my whole life?

What are we supposed to do about all of this, and how should we sustain his memory?

I'm starting to think the task before me is to live into this paradox, to carry these questions, to accept what can and cannot be changed, and to make friends with this God who invites my collaboration, but who won't wipe away all of my tears (at least not yet). And, quite in spite of myself, I'm starting to feel a little bit peaceful about it.

Walking Away

Being Held and Letting Go

On the anniversary of Will's death, a group of about thirty friends gather with us at a Benedictine monastery, to dedicate a tree at sunset and fill its branches with hand-painted wooden sparrows, and then to crowd into a tiny prayer chapel to remember him, and talk about what he taught us, and to pray to the One who gives and takes away.

In that stone structure lit by candles, I looked around at the people there and could finally see what had been there all along: love and support. Simple and precious things. These people whom I have privately pushed against, and silently accused of misunderstanding me, and toward whom I have felt bitterness, harboring silent grudges for healthy children and happy lives, and upon whom I have placed demands for empathy on my terms, in my time. These people are here on a Wednesday evening, having strained through traffic and sacrificed whatever comforts they would find at home, to be here. It is the great gift of *presence*, plain and simple. Most of them will not even speak or pray, and some of them will not even greet me. But they are here, bearing my burdens and sharing my sadness and loaning me their hope and faith and giving me their love. I look around to see their candlelit faces and rewind the last eighteen months and see that they haven't changed, but I have. I can finally see what was behind all their silence, awkwardness, and even their occasionally painful comments. All along, it has been love.

There's a similar silent space the day after the memorial as there was following the funeral. We say good-bye to everyone and send our family off on their daylong drive the next morning, and clean the big coffeepot and let our daughter collapse into an exhausted heap in her crib. Life feels more manageable now as we catch up on email and phone calls and cleaning, but it also feels a little lonely.

We're aware that we'll always observe September 12, but the observances will become increasingly quiet and small. This realization isn't as sad or forlorn or depressing as it might sound, for it is only fair and right that life go on, and that we release our friends and family from their holding of our memory, this holding of their breath. That we release them to go on to their own families, and that we look for ways to give back to them, and others. Sitting by the pool as the cool fall air mixes with the warm sun to make the perfect environment, I can look to my left at the place where we served him lunch alfresco, and I can smile instead of cry. I miss him, but I'm also glad for the memories, instead of tortured by them. I'm thankful for the time, instead of greedy for more. I'm trusting in the God who has walked with me, even as I'm wary of the same one who could have helped me but didn't.

In all of this, I have this strange sensation of becoming weaker and stronger at the same time. I have an awareness that I'll always be marked by this experience: that when someone I know is sick or dies, I'll feel these same scars and dip down into these same feelings. Yet at the same time I'll always have a quiet confidence about these great fears, an awareness that life includes bitter pain along with inexplicable beauty, and that death is not, finally, the last word. There is strength in weakness, and there is weakness in strength. And somehow, in all of it, there is hope.

Embodiment

My wife works as a nurse in a high-risk labor and delivery unit, which means that at the end of her day, she frequently has good news of a great day. However, it is sometimes the worst kind of news that drags her down. I know her well enough to see what kind of day she's just had (whether it be a day of life or a day of death) simply based on her stride when she walks out the door and heads to our car at the end of her twelve-hour shift.

Two days ago, her stride was heavy, and she quietly told me that she'd be going to a memorial service. A premature baby who had been treated in the neonatal intensive care unit for 126 days had died. What struck me was just how long that seemed, and we quietly contemplated what it meant for those parents to spend each of those days beside the bed of their beloved child, only to go home empty-handed.

Trying to get some perspective, we quickly added up the days of Will's life as we drove down Route 50 to our home, and as our daughter slept quietly in the back seat. Our eyebrows were at full salute when we added the twelve days of September to come to . . . 126 days. A very long time in one sense, yet painfully short in another.

My wife is there as I write this, at the very same funeral home where we took our first steps in planning a funeral, where our son's body was prepared, and where we visited to deliver his casket and fix his hair in preparation for the viewing. She is in that place to pay her respects to a bereaved family, and to honor the life of a child cut tragically short. My tendency is to process grief inside my head and in abstract, whereas my wife is painfully practical. She engages with other families who are living at this nexus of life and death, offering her very self to them. She's been anxious about this event all day, but she went anyway. As she walked down the stairs outside, I called from an open window to pass on the words that mattered most to me when our son died:

"Please tell them that their daughter's life mattered. . . ."

My 9/11

A poem, composed shortly before the first anniversary of Will's death on September 12, 2007:

> you never know
> the last, last, last
> until it has passed
>
> last laundry
> last meal
> last car ride
> last room
> last smile
> last diaper
> last cry
> last look
> last breath
>
> only in retrospect
> as you rewind
> do you realize
> that everything is different
> there's a big hole
> in your world
> an empty silence
> a searing pain

a tight ball of imponderables to untangle
a span of time that you didn't know was a lifetime

so you search for meaning
and breathe, and cry, and look
back to the kitchen, car, and laundromat, too

until something shifts
imperceptibly
the books call it "acceptance"
but it might be exhaustion
utter fatigue from asking the same questions
feeling the same pain
poring over the same emptiness
until your eyes can see
the beauty that was there all along

Walking On

Where do we go from here? I want to write something con-clusive or to at least set a goal of resolution that I can work toward. But there is no conclusion that I can imagine, because this journey doesn't end. And any resolution that I might work for would be false, because I suspect that there is no satisfying way to resolve the pain and disappointment I feel. Moreover, I don't *want* to conclude or resolve *anything*: both seem uncomfortably like they would involve forgetting my son, or ignoring what I've felt, or missing out on what I've learned and experienced. Worst of all, *concluding* and *resolving* both seem as though they would domesticate God, who has walked with me through all of this as a friend and co-laborer, rather than some genie in a snake-oil bottle. No, I want to pick up the pieces of my new life, put them in my bag, and walk on.

When I close my eyes, I remember his eyes—those deep eyes that would gaze into mine with that wise, knowing earnestness. But in particular, I remember that calm middle-distance stare I saw on his last night; I remember the almost grainy appearance of his corneas in the dusky light of that hospital room. It was the last look he gave me before his breathing halted and his heart stopped. Was he looking at me, or past me, or through me, somehow? I wonder if, in that moment, he was seeing the tunnel slowly close in around him and was in fact moving to the other side, into a fuller life in God.

I'm right behind you, my son, my brother, my friend, my hero.

Treasure

May 2009

in the center of my chest
is a particle
an irritant
like a piece of sand,
only bigger

it rises up
when I'm sad
twists
when I'm lonely
rubs
at birthdays
burns
when I pray

it's never going to go away
I know that now
it'll always be there
choking my throat
catching my breath
constraining my heart

but somehow,
like an oyster
I will slowly encase it
in layers of milky coating
to make it smoother
rounder
more beautiful

and when my flesh
is put to flame
and the man
sweeps up my old bones
that tiny pearl
will roll into the dust bin
he'll squint,
the crease of his eye
turned up into a slight smile
wondering where it came
    from

Notes

Leg Cramps

Ryan Lee Sharp, *In Search of a Unified Theory* [CD], The Cobalt Season. Produced and Recorded by Ryan Lee Sharp and Daniel Dixon (2007). Since Ryan is a close friend, there are several songs here that have some connection to our experience, including "Brighter Skies, an Advent Song" and "Careful Not to Draw Your Maps in Pen and Ink." But my favorite is probably still "Begin Again."

In the section Medical Missionaries, Michael Ruhlman's breathtaking book *Walk on Water: The Miracle of Saving Children's Lives* (New York: Penguin Books, 2003) was a great help. This is a compelling overview of the work of pediatric cardiac units, as well as the adventurously experimental history of pediatric cardiac surgery. Ruhlman is a widely revered writer on food and cooking, but this spellbinding departure from his forte had my heart racing and my eyes on the verge of tears for three hundred pages.

Middle-Distance Stare

John D. Caputo, *The Weakness of God: A Theology of the Event* (Bloomington: Indiana University Press, 2006). Dr. Caputo is a world-class postmodern theologian, and I won't claim that I understood every word of this book. But his freedom from theological strictures and his very pastoral perspective give him a unique and important voice.

Jürgen Moltmann, *The Crucified God: The Cross of Christ as the Foundation and Criticism of Christian Theology* (New York: Harper & Row, 1974). I was privileged to sit down with Professor Moltmann as a public interlocutor at the Emergent Village Theological Conversation (September 2009) and speak to him about theodicy and grief. His humane, pastoral, and brilliant insights have informed my thoughts here and eased my pain. Dr. Moltmann is a rare combination of theological genius and scarred human vessel; he does his work with a broken heart.

Crossing the Line

Lauren Winner, *Mudhouse Sabbath* (Brewster, MA: Paraclete Press, 2003). My thanks to the random person who heard my story at a meeting and quietly recommended the chapter on grief from this book that had helped him so much in his loss.

Doug Pagitt, *A Christianity Worth Believing: Hope-Filled, Open-Armed, Alive-and-Well Faith for the Left Out, Left Behind, and Let Down in Us All* (San Francisco: Jossey-Bass, 2008). Although Doug's book wasn't published until after I completed my writing, I was privileged to read the developing manuscript several times during my year of grief. Doug has written many good books, but this one is his best. My thoughts in the section Theodicy were very much informed by his.

Elisabeth Kübler-Ross, *On Death and Dying* (New York: Routledge, 1969). Another book that was extremely helpful to me: Alan D. Wolfelt's *Understanding Your Grief: Ten Essential Touchstones for Finding Hope and Healing Your Heart* (Chicago: Companion Press, 2004). If I had read it more carefully, I would have been disabused of my misconception that Dr. Kübler-Ross's stages were strictly chronological. Wolfelt states: "[Kübler-Ross] lists the five stages of grief that she saw terminally ill patients experience in the face of their own impending death: denial, anger, bargaining, depression, and acceptance. However, Kübler-Ross never intended for her stages to be interpreted as a rigid, linear sequence to be followed by all mourners. Readers, however, have done just that, and the consequences have often been disastrous" (24).